Prepper's Guide to Survival Off the Grid

How to Plan and Execute Living off the Grid

Jack Bright

Table of Contents:

What Is Off-Grid Living? 7

Why Should You Live Off-Grid? 8

Roughing It 10

How to Pick the Right Off-Grid Home for You 24

Can You Live Anywhere? 25

How to Pick the Right Area 26

Log Cabin 31

Yurt 33

Sustainable Cob Home 34

Timber Frame Cabin 36

Straw Bale Home 37

Stick Frame House 39

Trailers and RV Homes 40

Underground Home 41

Choosing the Best Plants to Grow 43

Schedule Planting 46

Irrigation System 48

Protecting the Garden 50

Seed Saving or Seed Crops 50

Chickens 55

Bees 57

Goats 58

Pigs 59

Sheep 60

Cows 61

Geese 62

Ducks 63

Quail 64

Fish 64

Rabbits 65

Food Preservation for Off Grid Dwellers 67

Canning 68

Smoking, Salting, or Drying 70

How Do Rural Homes Generally Source Their Water? 74

Alternative Water Systems for Off Grid Living 77

Off-Grid Water Storage 80

Water Contamination 82

Building a Bio-Filter 83

Building a UV Water Purification System 85

Ceramic Water Filtration 87

Chemical Disinfectants 89

Distillation for Water Purification 89

Boiling for Water Purification 90

Off Grid Solar Energy 92

Designing Your Solar System 93

Determine the Size of Your Solar System 96

Determining the Amount of Solar Energy Produced 98

Hydro Electric and Micro Hydro in an Off-Grid Home 102

Determining The Amount of Water Power That Can Be Generated 105

How to Construct a Micro-Hydro Inlet 108

The Difference between a Buried and Above Ground Penstock 109

Building the Turbine House 110

Using Hydropower with a Grid Connected Power System 113

Off Grid Air Conditioning 114

Alternatives for Septic Systems in Your Off Grid Home............................ 122

Rent a House or Land.. 127

Land Partners.. 128

Communities 128

Building or Finding a Tiny Off-Grid Home... 129

Renting Off-Grid Land.. 129

Is Off-Grid Living Meant for You?

The concept of off-grid living is becoming more and more popular, and this is because of the rewarding lifestyle that comes with it. You may have probably heard about off-grid living and suddenly feel like you want to try it for yourself. But is it really meant for you? Living closer to nature seems quite novel and amazing, but not everyone is suited for the off-grid lifestyle, and that's okay. It's important that you first cover every detail of what this kind of lifestyle entails and what you need to do, and most importantly if this is something that you can realistically manage on a regular basis.

Instead of romanticizing the idea of it, it is better to learn and acknowledge the challenges of this change in lifestyle first. It has advantages and disadvantages, and you have to weigh them against your needs and preferences. Maybe you really are meant to leave the hustle and bustle of the city behind and move off-grid. Maybe you should stick to the urban lifestyle and try making smaller changes that will help improve your quality of life without giving up on modern conveniences.

What Is Off-Grid Living?

Living off-grid is not the same for everyone but can usually be summarized quite simply. Off- grid living is a way of life that generally means you have to give up on the modern conveniences of the Internet, electricity, and technology. You don't have to camp under the stars, but you do need to live away from urban areas. You can build or buy a home to live in, but you will have to fend for most of your needs yourself. Some people choose to live away from other people, while others choose to join off-grid communities with like-minded people.

It is not just about disconnecting from the modern world but about learning to provide for
yourself in a self-sufficient way. You will have to learn to grow your own food, obtain yourwater yourself and even generate electricity. Off-grid living makes you more self-reliant thanyou would ever have expected yourself to be. And if you're not someone who can learn to do everything yourself, this lifestyle might just not be for you.

Off-grid living involves:

- Generating your own electricity
- Sourcing water by yourself
- Home-schooling your kids
- Living without the internet
- Growing your own food
- Rearing animals for meat or dairy
- Learning to tend to minor medical issues yourself

- Waste management
- And more

Why Should You Live Off-Grid?

You may still need a bit of convincing since it takes a lot of work to go off-grid. Here are some reasons why you should try off-grid living.

To Save Money

When you first move to an off-grid location, it will require an initial investment. However, it saves you a lot of money in the long run. Investing in solar panels or wind energy is definitely cheaper than paying huge amounts on electricity bills your whole life. However, even if youdon't choose to live completely off-grid, you will still save money by making other changes.

To Reconnect with Nature

With urban living, most of us have lost touch with nature. We're so caught up in lives that are dictated by technology and innovation, that we've left nature behind and no longer connect with it. Very few people even have the time to grow some plants on the balconies. When you leavethe noise and pollution of the city behind, you get the opportunity to immerse yourself in nature again. Living in a more country setting will help you connect with the environment around you. When you grow your own food or rear some animals, it will bring you closer to nature. You can experience sleeping with the stars above and waking up with the sunrise. You won't spend hours immersed in technology and will have the opportunity to watch the birds or sit near the river.

To Leave behind the Stress of Urban Living

The modern lifestyle can be very hectic and stressful. It takes a toll on the body and mind andcan be too much for most people. By going off-grid, you can leave the stressful hustle behindand live a better slow-paced life. Living in the old way can be so much better than the life we now live.

To Become More Self-Sufficient

Have you tried living without your phone for a day? Or with the power being cut because you haven't paid the bill on time? These are all instances that show you just how dependent you areon modern technology and amenities. If you want to be more self-sufficient and less reliant on others, you need to go off-grid.

To Promote Sustainability

Think of how you live your life currently. How much water do you waste or use right now? Howoften do you use plastic to carry your groceries home? How much time do you spend on your phone? All of us in the modern world are big consumers in every way and very wasteful. If you care about a sustainable lifestyle and would like to leave the world a little better for future generations, off-grid living can contribute greatly to this. Not only does it help you consume less,but it also helps you produce more. You learn to replace a lot of what you use. You learn to fix things and not just throw them away. It is a lot less stressful on the environment than urban living, which exhausts resources and generates too much waste.

To Challenge Yourself

If you are just looking for a way to live life more excitingly and love taking up challenging projects, this can be quite fun. You will learn how to do almost every single thing on your own and be self-sufficient as you adapt to an off-grid lifestyle. It is also a great way to teach your children how to live a better way. Living off-grid gives you a sense of achievement as you rely on yourself and nature. You contribute to the world and also encourage others to live in a better way. You learn to adapt outside your comfort zone.

It isn't necessary to completely rough it and live like our ancestors. You can try off-grid living in a few different ways.

Roughing It

This is the most intensive way of choosing to live the off-grid lifestyle. In this case, you have to go completely off-grid and cannot rely on any technology or government services. You need to find your own water source, build a septic tank to dispose of waste, and use only renewable energy sources such as solar energy. In fact, you can even choose to live completely without electricity. You will have to grow your own food in a garden and rear animals. You will have to build your own toilet and just about figure everything out for yourself. Off-grid living in this way is quite difficult and is popular amongst people who like challenges and can survive extreme situations. It has advantages since you will save so much money and have almost no bills to pay again. You also reconnect with nature and learn to survive with minimal resources. The trouble is, you will be completely cut off from any modern amenities, and it can take time to get used to this complete level of self-reliance.

Half Off-Grid

This means that you don't have to rough it completely and can use certain essential amenities even while going off-grid to a large extent. You will be learning more self-reliance, but you don't have to completely forsake amenities such as the municipal sewer system. Instead, you focus more on growing your own food or using solar panels. The degree of self-reliance you embrace will be up to you, and this is easier than completely roughing it. An advantage is that you will greatly reduce costs compared to urban living, and another is that you can actually try off-grid living without completely switching to it. The disadvantage is that you cannot completely achieve the purpose of being self-reliant through off-grid living.

Modern Off-Grid

This is the easiest and most popular way of adapting to the off-grid lifestyle. This means that you don't have to give up on modern amenities but still learn to be more self-reliant. For instance, you don't have to live without electricity but have to harness it with solar or wind power. You need to set up a pump for getting water, and you also have to build a septic tank. You will be putting systems in place to help you live more comfortably in a modern way. You can also still use appliances such as refrigerators if you want. Despite having these amenities, you can be more self-reliant by growing your own food and trying more DIY solutions around the house. This off-grid lifestyle is a lot easier to adapt for most people used to the modern lifestyle. It still helps you save a lot of money in the long run, but you will have to spend a large amount on setting everything up first.

Considering that off-grid living can be a very big decision, you must be practical about your chosen approach. Don't try to rough it when you are someone who heavily relies on urban facilities. Choosing any of the three ways of an off-grid lifestyle will still have a positive impact. The more you learn to rely on yourself, the better. But the degree of it can vary for each person, and that is perfectly acceptable.

Chapter Two
Making a Plan

Once you decide that you want to try off-grid living, you need to start making a plan. It's not a choice you can casually make or execute. If you just jump in with no plan, it might be much more difficult to get things done and successfully transition to an off-grid lifestyle. If you are an urban dweller considering off-grid living, start preparing before making the jump.

Enlighten Yourself

Get as much information on off-grid living as possible. The first thing to do is to read up on everything you can about off-grid living. This book is your first stop, but there is a lot of information to help you along the way. Go on forums where other off-grid dwellers or enthusiasts share their experiences and issues. All of this will go a long way in helping you prepare.

Be Realistic

It is very important to be realistic when considering off-grid living. First off, think of the money. If you want to rough it, you must invest some money to set yourself up first. It takes money to setup solar panels, a new house, etc. Can you afford what you are considering? What are your other options? You need to know your own limitations as well and not take on more than you can handle.

Take a Look at Different Locations

When considering building or buying an off-grid home, you need to look at many details. Look into the climate of that area and whether you will be able to live comfortably there. What are the building code requirements and taxes applicable? Look at the land availability and landholding options as well. All of these are important factors in picking the best location for your off-grid home. The cost of moving, building or buying in that location matters. If you plan to continue working at your current job and have to commute, will it be feasible? Will your children be able to commute to school or college if you don't plan on homeschooling them? Also, considering thatyou might not live near the best roadways, you might have to invest in a better vehicle that is more suitable for such terrain.

Consider Housing Options

Once you pick the location, you have to think about whether you want to buy or build there. Are there any cabins that you can buy? Do you want to build a small or big house? How many peoplewill be living there? The more people, the more energy and resources you will need. What arethe materials you will need for building? How much will they cost, and how easily are they available? Look around at the other off-grid houses in the location you are considering. Consider the pros and cons of any housing options. Transport, cost, durability, etc., will all impact your shelter options.

Look at the Energy Options

You will need energy for various needs such as heating, cooling, or cooking. Consider thevarious options for off-grid energy supply. You may choose to still connect with the government's electricity network, which is also okay. However, it might be best to consider renewable sources if you want to go off-grid. This includes anything from solar, wind, windmills, and generators. The size of the house, your needs, and location will affect your poweror energy options.

Water Availability

Ideally, you will have a natural water source near your off-grid home. If not, you will have to consider everything from good drilling to water delivery. You also need to consider whether it will be easy to haul or pump water in that location. Since water is an essential need, it is one of the first factors to consider when moving to an off-grid location. It needs to be a practical decision since lack of water later can be a huge issue. The water quality is very important since you will be drinking it, so make sure you insert a good filter system.

Food Supply Options

If you intend to rough it and not live in an urban area, you need to grow and rear your food and meat. Do you have the skills to hunt, grow, fish, etc.? If not, you may want to pick up on these skills during preparation. Remember to check the licensing requirements and laws in the region for such activities. They will come in handy later and make you more self-sufficient regarding food. Learn the basics of growing vegetables, grains, etc., so you don't have to go buy them. Build up your skills in this as much as possible since growing your own food is one of the most essential skills of off-grid living. Consider the amount of food you need to grow per person. Think of the climate and soil and what you will be able to grow. Also, learn more about food preservation since you will need supplies for the winter. When you have excess produce, you canalways try fermentation, canning, pickling, etc.

Making Money

How will you be making money? Even if you want to go off-grid, you will need money. Unless you have a large amount saved away or some pension income that will come in, you need an income source. You may choose to continue with your current job, but if not, you need to consider other moneymaking options. If you want to be completely off-grid, you can try selling some of the produce you grow or the meat you rear. You can also try making natural products with your resources, such as essential oils, tea blends, natural beauty products, etc. Sell at the local farmer's market or online if you choose to have access to the Internet. Financial self- sufficiency is also important in off-grid living.

First Aid Skills

When you live in an off-grid location, the nearest clinic, pharmacy or hospital will usually be a little far away. However, you will still find yourself having to deal with common ailments and injuries. Learn as many first aid skills as possible so you can take care of yourself and your family in such situations. It will go a long way in helping you minimize the issue until you can reach the nearest medical facility.

Networking

Chances are, there are other people living off-grid near you. Be friendly and get to know your neighbors. It will help you learn a lot from their personal experiences. It will also be a way in which you can exchange resources. If you grow certain vegetables, you can barter with them for what they grow or have an excess of. Joining online communities before you move will also give you a lot of knowledge and help you prepare.

Make a Supply List

Start making a list to prepare yourself before you make the actual move. This should include everything from building materials like tools or wood and fishing or gardening equipment. Buy in bulk for what you will need a lot of and stock up on things that have a long shelf life. Don't forget medication and fill up your first aid kit. Do your research and prepare for off-grid living properly before you do the actual deed. Hopefully, the information given throughout the book will help you prepare as thoroughly as possible.

Here is a checklist to get started with your off-grid lifestyle:

Become Debt Free

The first thing to focus on is to go debt free. If you want to live a free life and go off-grid, you need to get rid of unwanted ties; this is especially important with debt. Once you pay off all your debt, you can use your savings to move to an off-grid home with no worries. Start by writing all your income, expenses, and debt down. Slowly pay everything off even while you are saving. Setting up a monthly budget and cutting down on any unnecessary expenses will go a long way.

Learn New Skills

Once you pay off your debt, or even while you do this, start picking up new skills. A self- sufficient off-grid lifestyle is not for someone who cannot get things done. There are so many skills that will come in once you move to an off-grid home. Some skills to try learning during the preparation phase include canning, woodcutting, cooking, gardening, foraging, etc. There are so many tutorials online, and you will find many workshops in your area as well. Take advantage of these resources and pick up as many skills as possible.

Look for the Best Location

Finding land might be the biggest problem for off-grid moves. In the next section, you will learn more about finding the perfect location. However, you need to sit and set a budget first. Look at your savings and get an estimate of how much you can spend on buying land or on putting a down payment. There is no point in wandering around looking at places you can't afford. Youcan then think about which state or locality you would like to move to. Take your time to find theright location and good affordable land. You might find that talking to people and going ononline forums is more helpful than just looking at listings or asking real estate agents. Once you find the perfect land, negotiate and close at the price you can afford.

Meet the Water Needs

Once you buy an off-grid property, work on developing the water source. This is the most basic human need, and you will need water for everything from drinking and cooking to possibly generating power. If a natural water source is present on the property, you will find off-gridliving a lot more convenient. Figure out your water needs, and then plan on how to meet these requirements. You may have to set up a rainwater collection system alongside a water purification system for water from the spring.

Construct a House

Once you buy a property and figure out your needs, start building the off-grid house of your dreams. It could be anything as simple as a yurt to a large log cabin. A well-built home will keep you and your family safe and comfortable even when you go off-grid. Have a budget set for this as well, and be realistic about how much you can do alone. Hiring professionals or buying a house is better if you don't have the right skills. You will be living there for a long time, and building an inefficient house will only cause problems. You might have to do things by yourself if you choose a natural building process. It is easy to hire professionals for stick frame homes or brick houses. Have a temporary arrangement for housing until the permanent off-grid house is completed. This could be a tent or even an RV. Check the local laws and regulations, get the building permits, and start building.

Waste Management

Another important aspect of off-grid living that you need to focus on is waste management. While you set up the house, you need to figure out methods for efficiently managing waste. You may need to plan this out before the house is constructed since some elements must be factored into the plans for the building. Get the outhouse, septic system, composting toilet, etc., set up alongside as the house is being built. Also, make sure you have a plan for how this waste management system will be handled over time. For instance, if you have a septic tank, it will need to be pumped out and cleaned every few years.

Heating or Cooling

One of the major costs or power-consuming aspects of a house is heating and cooling. Think of the weather or climate in your area and plan the design of the house in a way that you can take advantage of free ways to heat or cool the house. You should determine where the windows should be placed, so temperatures don't get too high. You can implement the use of thermal masses to keep the house at normal temperatures too. Other than these free heating or cooling methods, take note of any other methods you may need to use. For instance, if you still need an air conditioner, it will have to be factored in while setting up the power system.

Set Up the Power System

First, you have to figure out all your power needs. This should include everything from lights to heating or cooling. You can set up an off-grid power system once you know your family's power needs. Instead of staying connected to the grid, opt for solar, wind, or micro-hydro power. These alternative power systems are better suited for the off-grid lifestyle. Consider the resources available to you, such as the amount of sunlight throughout the year or the water flow from the river nearby. If you live in a windy area, you can tap into wind power too. Instead of depending on a single power source, supplement a primary source with a secondary one. One of the best options is to set up a solar power system with a micro hydro system. This can be a very efficient power system set up for off-grid dwellers.

Grow Your Own Food

Now that you have your house, water and power need to be met, start growing your own food. Choose the right spot to start planting and get started. You need to know how much food youwill need for yourself or your family and plant accordingly. This will give you an estimate of your yearly crop goal. Then plan out the garden so you will be able to grow as much food as you can or need efficiently. Fix the soil, so you have rich land to work with. Set up a fence to keep animals or people out. Set up an irrigation system for watering all the plants. Develop a calendar for planting and harvesting. Start with plants that are easy to grow but maintain variety since you will be relying on your garden for your dietary needs.

Raise Livestock

While this isn't essential if you don't eat meat or need dairy, it is recommended. Animals can be a great addition to an off-grid homestead. You can keep them for meat, milk, and manure and to protect the garden from pests. Start with livestock that doesn't require too much work, and then move your way to bigger animals. Chickens, goats, and pigs are a great few animals to start with.

Store or Preserve Food

Once you harvest your plants, you will have to wait until the new planting season arrives. You need to have food stored or preserved for the winter months. Picking up skills such as canning and having a freezer or root cellar are ways to be prepared for the colder season. You can always go to the store when you need food, but it is always best to keep yourself as self-sufficient as possible. While planting, remember to plant enough for food storage needs to be met as well.

If you go through this checklist along the way, you will soon be an expert at off-grid living.

How to Pick the Right Off-Grid Home for You

As off-grid homes have become increasingly popular, you will find thousands if not millions of listings online. If you want to buy a home and not build one, you are definitely going to be spoiled for choice. You can live in a cabin, yurt, tiny home, earth house, or something unique you choose to build. But if you haven't lived off the grid before, you may be confused about picking the right off-grid home for you. Here's some advice on that.

First, think carefully about what you want and what you need. These are not always the same, and you need to consider them properly. You need to be careful about noting such things since buying the wrong home or property can be a very expensive mistake you will want to avoid. Make a wise decision by considering your and your family's needs carefully.

Think of why you want to live off-grid as well. Knowing your reasons makes it easier to pick the best home or property for your off-grid lifestyle. Each person can have a unique reason for wanting to go off-grid. If you are a survivalist, you will want a different home than someone who wants to go off-grid just to save money or someone who wants a break from the noise and pollution of the city.

You may also be someone who wants to try homesteading and doesn't have the capital to buy a large enough property in urban areas. In this case, an off-grid property might be a good idea. You could be trying to be more minimal with everything, and this is another reason many people move off-grid. Write down your reasons and consider the options. Not everyone who moves off the grid likes living in a basic home. You can also build a big, beautiful home with all the off-grid luxury options you want. It would entirely depend on your needs and wants.

Can You Live Anywhere?

Consider the fact that reality and fantasies are usually quite far apart. You may have a certain idea about off-grid living in your home. Just looking at pictures of beautiful cabins in the woods is not enough. You might have to burn a fire for heat and fish or forage for food. Think of the reality of the situation in depth and consider whether you can meet the demands of an off-grid life. Unless you are single and want to cut yourself off from society, consider a location that will still allow you access to schools, work, or hospital without too much of a hassle. A completely remote location is not for everyone. And for a beginner at off-grid living, it can be even more difficult. Don't expect yourself to learn how to be completely self-sufficient in one go. Keep your options open by living a little closer to civilization instead of buying a tiny home in the mountains.

How to Pick the Right Area

Everyone wants to find the ideal spot for their off-grid home, one where you can achieve all yourself-sufficient, off-grid dreams. The property has to be such that it is practical and still fulfills your ideals. You can't just pick a spot in the middle of nowhere and cut yourself off from the world. This would be impractical and might cause issues later, especially if you have a family to consider. Some places are actually a lot harder to live in than other off-grid spots. You need to take time to evaluate the pros and cons of each space. Making a list of your important criteria will help you pick the right property. It should be practical and allow you to live on your terms without too much discomfort.

Off-grid living is not easy by any means, but you probably aren't looking for an easy way out either. After all, the conveniences of modern living would be much easier. However, if you don't keep some factors in mind while picking your off-grid property, your life will soon be a lot more difficult than you might want it to be. It would prevent you from enjoying your newfound freedom and instead make you regret the move in the first place. To avoid this, you need to take the right approach to pick the perfect off-grid location for your home.

Vital Services Need to Be Accessible

You don't need to give up on vital services such as hospitals just to live off-grid. Many locations suitable for isolated living are still near developed urban areas. You can be prepared with first aidkits, but a lot of medical issues need serious medical attention. You wouldn't want to live hours away from the nearest health care facility in emergencies. This is especially important if youhave children or elderly people living with you. You can be as self-sufficient as you want, but 100% is not possible since you still need help in such cases. Try to live within a couple of miles of the nearest hospital if possible.

Easily Available Natural Resources

You need to check if the property gives you access to many natural resources. This is essentialfor off-grid living since you will have to make the best of what is available in nature. If you intend to rough it, this is especially important. If you plan on using solar panels for energy, you need to ensure that you live in a place that gets a lot of sunlight throughout the year. If you want to use water turbines, you will need to live near a river or some such resource that will allow youto make use of this. You also need a good water source for your regular water supply. Check the rules and regulations in the area as well since there might be restrictions on what you can and can't do. For instance, you might not be allowed to hunt in certain places.

Is the Land Fertile?

When you intend to grow your own food, you need to live on fertile land. If you buy a property with completely barren land or there are issues such as lack of water, you will not be able togrow anything there. Infertile soil can always be fixed, but there are limits, and it can be expensive to have to fix everything. If the property doesn't get enough sunlight or water, it willbe very difficult to grow vegetables for regular consumption. You can always go to town to stockup on some supplies, but you can't be self-sufficient if you can't grow at least some of your food.

Affordability

A very important factor to consider is what you can or cannot afford. You need to have a budget in mind and look at properties that will fall within that budget. Some places are very expensive while others can help you save a lot. You can even look around and find an affordable property that others haven't discovered yet. Don't take a loan or spend all your savings on your off-grid home. Money is always important, especially if you have children. Buy a property you can affordwithout compromising your family's or your own future.

Check the Climate

The climate of a region is a factor you have no control over. You may want a cabin in the mountains, but it is going to be a challenge to live there when the weather gets very cold. You need to heat the house constantly, and your gardening will also come to a standstill. If theseasons are feasible, you won't be able to grow any plants for most of the year. It can also be an issue if it is too hot since you may not be very tolerant to the heat. You have to know if you can keep your home cool or hot as needed without relying too much on the temperature regulating systems. Ideally, you should pick a place with a mild climate where the winters aren't too harsh, and the summers are too hot. You don't want to be sweating half the year and shoveling snow forthe rest of it.

Development Plans

You can go off-grid in a sparsely populated area but should look at the development plans for thenearby areas. It is ideal since you would have access to what you need even while you live in isolation. That way, if you ever want to go for dinner at a restaurant or need to buy supplies, you will have things nearby.

Building Codes and Zoning Laws

The zoning laws and local building codes need to be taken into account. These will dictate whether you can even live or build on a particular property. These will also determine what kind of home you can build there. The more lax the codes are, the better it is for you. This will allow you to build the off-grid home of your dreams. The zoning laws will determine if you areallowed to cut any trees or park an RV there. Look into all this to avoid any issues in the future.

Septic System

Check for waste disposal solutions. Most places have rules and regulations on how waste has to be disposed of. Even if you intend to use a composting or alternative toilet, you will need to set up an appropriate septic system for any wastewater. Ask around for suggestions from neighboring off-grid dwellers and the local municipality.

Property Taxes or Fees

While the cost of buying the actual property is the main concern, you also need to consider property taxes or fees. Look at the applicable taxes in each location. The real estate listings in most places will display these details. You need to factor this in when you consider the overall cost of an off-grid home.

Chapter Four
Off Grid Housing Options

If you want to explore more options than just buying a house in an off-grid location, there's a lot more than you might have expected. Buying a house can be quite expensive, and building one might often be the better option. You might not have heard of these off-grid housing options before, but they are simple and very cost-effective. Not only will you save money, but they also have their own advantages as compared to commercial homes for an off-grid lifestyle. This section will introduce you to these housing options and help you weigh the pros and cons as well.

Log Cabin

When you first think of living off-grid, log cabins usually come to mind. Mankind has beenliving in log cabins for centuries, and there are many reasons why our ancestors built them in the past. They are easy to build, durable, and can be quite comfortable. If you buy a property with many trees, you can use the wood to build a modern version of a log cabin for yourself and your family. It will save you a lot of money compared to commercial houses and doesn't really requiretoo much work. The skills required for building log cabins are easy enough for anyone to pick upand hard as complicated as modern carpentry. You can also invest in a few hand tools that will come in handy over the long term.

A common myth is that a log cabin is never insulated. This is not true at all. An insulated wall in the usual modern home is usually R-20. The insulation value is a little lower per inch for wood. However, the thicker the wood you use, the higher the insulation will be. And these are almost always thicker than the typical 6" walls in urban homes. An average log cabin constructed with 20" thick logs can easily have insulation of around R30. Thus you can build a log cabin that might be more insulated than typical houses in the city. You can always supplement this insulation factor by installing rigid foam into the walls.

Another misconception about log cabins is that it is a waste of wood. It may seem like these cabins require a lot of extra wood, but it isn't true. A normal wood-framed house would actually cause more wastage because a lot of trimming and sawing is involved. This means cutting wood and sawdust causes more wastage, and this isn't a real issue with log cabins where whole pieces are used. In fact, the average log cabin would use about as much wood as is used in a normal stick frame house. If you want to contribute to the conservation of the environment, try using wood from your own property or locally. It adds to your carbon footprint if you get it shipped from lumberyards far away.

So, if you are interested in a log cabin, find a practical builders guide and learn how to do it yourself. You could also hire professionals to do this for you, and it would still cost less than hiring modern construction laborers for cement homes. There are a lot of manuals and online videos that provide step-by-step instructions on successfully building your own off-grid log cabin.

Yurt

Consider living in a yurt if you want a very cheap option for your off-grid home. These are large and round tent-like structures that serve as semi-permanent homes. If you want the option to move at any time and travel or just aren't sure about off-grid living, this might be a good choice. These yurts are originally from Asia and were built to survive extremely cold weather. They are surprisingly durable and very light. The original structures were built using natural materials like wood, animal skin, etc.. Still, modern yurt construction involves the use of wooden beams for a lattice and canvas or vinyl for the walls. You can buy a readymade yurt structure online within a price range of $1000-$20,000. The price will vary according to the structure and material. However, if you have skilled hands, you can also create a yurt yourself using the right materials. A little sewing and woodworking will be enough.

One disadvantage to consider is that yurts are inexpensive structures but require extra heating when you live in a cold climate. In a traditional yurt, people had open fires inside, and the roof of the tent would have an opening to allow the smoke to leave. In a modern yurt, off-grid dwellers opt for a wood stove or even a rocket mass heater.

Sustainable Cob Home

Let's talk about cob homes now. Most people don't know about cob building, but it is a great option for an off-grid home. These structures are easy to build and quite versatile. The construction involves an affordable earth-based technique that allows you to live in a home with solid walls. If you aren't familiar with cob, it is a mixture of plant fiber, clay, and soil. Once mixed, these materials will be kneaded into a dough-like consistency. This cob is then molded to build free-form walls for a house.

It is a very environmentally friendly material since everything is easily sourced from your own property or can be obtained easily. Each component of a cob home is cheap and found anywhere in the country. The technique of building with cob is also very easy and a skill that any beginner can master. You don't have to be physically strong to handle the materials either, unlike the physical effort required with bricks and cement.

You may be concerned about moisture issues when you think about cob building. However, this is actually not a problem, and cob houses will not usually leave you with moisture-related issues.

You may find that cob walls are better at handling moisture than the walls of many modern buildings. This is because the material is partially permeable and acts like a buffer while allowing moisture movement instead of retaining it. Your cob home will be efficient in balancing moisture levels instead of creating an unhealthy moist environment within. This is a natural way of dehumidification or humidification in an off-grid home. Cob homes are better suited for dry or slightly moist climates and can last a long time. They are also a form of sustainable housing.

Cob-style homes can be found all over the world and are quite long lasting. They are sturdy natural homes that will not be ruined if built properly. It is important to have a proper stem wall since that will help protect the house from any direct rain damage. If your region is prone to a lot of heavy rainfall that might often strike the walls of your house, a little maintenance work from time to time will be required. To do this, you will have to do some refinishing on the earth's plaster exteriors. However, this task rarely takes more than a few hours and is very feasible. If you want to protect the walls from rain with an extra measure, use limestone plaster to finish the exterior walls. However, you need to avoid using any materials that are impervious to water. Something like concrete plaster will actually trap moisture within the wall and cause serious damage to your cob home.

An advantage of a cob off-grid home is its natural heating and cooling characteristics. Similar to a cave, the interiors will be cool during the summer months and retain warmth during cold wintermonths. The overall insulation levels are not very high, but the design of a cob home makes it suitable for living. In fact, the inside of a cob home will be more comfortable during a hot summer afternoon than any wood or concrete house.

So, it is a sustainable option if you want to try cob building in your off-grid adventure. Get a few books with modern updates on cob building, and you can use the technique to build a comfortable home for yourself. You can even sign up for a cob-building course and pick up the necessary skills before venturing on it alone.

Timber Frame Cabin

These cabins are a blend of log cabins and stick frame homes. They are becoming increasingly popular in the off-grid community these days. The technique used in constructing these cabins involves the use of large beams of timber, and traditional methods of wood joining are used instead of nailing. This construction method has been carried out in a few variations for centuries worldwide. Century-old Pagodas in Japan were constructed using this method too and are still standing.

Timber frames can be built using timber harvested from trees on your property or from local suppliers. While this is an advantage with log cabins, there is a little extra prep work involved. Inlog cabins, the wooden logs can be used directly. However, the ones used in timber frame construction have to be milled first. This building technique allows you to construct more modern houses, and there is a lot more flexibility in designing. An off-grid home built with timber frames often suit modern tastes because they can easily be made to look like a regular urban house. But if you want a more rustic appearance, you have the flexibility to achieve such designs as well. Another benefit is that timber frame houses can be built with engineer-approved designs and are much easier to resell than many off-grid home designs. These structures can be built following legal construction codes and thus can be mortgaged as well.

You don't have to spend much time getting the house built when you opt for timber framing. Once you get the required materials, the process can be completed relatively fast, and you soon have a house you can live in. In fact, if you hire some extra help and the house is not too big, a timber frame house can even be built in a day or two. Taking a few practical classes on it first is recommended if you want to try doing this yourself. This will equip you with the necessary skills so you can get it right the first time. Some woodworking skills are necessary for timber frame techniques. But even if you have no experience, you can learn in a short period with a little guidance.

Straw Bale Home

If the thought of an earth home appeals to your mind, straw bale homes are another option to consider. Like a cob home, you will be using environmentally friendly materials, and everything is easily accessible. There are some advantages of opting for a straw bale home over cob homes that you might prefer as well. In a straw bale house, you will have to stack up square straw bales over each other, forming the core of your walls. The structural integrity of cob homes comes from the earth mixture. Thick layers of earth plaster are used in straw bale houses, which have to be spread in and over the straw. This will allow the straw to be permanently sealed and effectively protect the walls from the elements while providing structural integrity. The latter is better than cob walls since the construction time is shorter and there is more insulation value. There is dead air space within straw bale walls, and this increases the insulation value. Thus, straw bale houses will also be a better option than some others for places where the winters can get very cold.

National building codes tend to be implemented in most states and have to be considered. Another advantage to consider is that straw bale building is one of the few natural building techniques that is accepted in national building codes. The building codes will specify slightly different methods than what natural builders use. This will usually require you to use a little stick framing with normal straw bale building since it allows better support for upper floors or the roof. And by adding this to your plans, it becomes easier for you to get a permit to build an off- grid straw bale home on your property.

Stick Frame House

While you have all these other options, a standard stick frame house might just be your preference, which will do nicely for an off-grid home. These stick frame houses are actually a preference for many people moving from urban homes to off-grid locations. Building the stick frame house alone is an option for someone highly motivated to do everything themselves. You might find the challenge quite fulfilling once you successfully complete it.

It will also save you a lot of money compared to buying one or getting others to make it for you. Another way to save money is to visit building sites and accumulate scrap materials you can reuse for your home. The size of the house itself will depend on how many people will be living in it. If you intend to build a tiny home, you can choose between a solid foundation and one on wheels. Many people choose to build off-grid stick frame homes on wheels since it gives them the freedom to move around. In this case, you can live off-grid without actually buying any land. Most places have tiny home communities where you can park your house for free or by paying a certain amount. If you are an outdoorsy person, you can build a tiny home with this construction technique and keep it within 100-300 sq ft. This will be much easier to travel with and allow you to live a minimalist grid lifestyle.

So, if you are motivated enough, you can easily watch some online tutorials or attend a few workshops to learn how to build a stick frame house yourself. It will help you learn how to set up everything from the frame of the house to plumbing. This is one of the best ways to be self- sufficient as far as possible in your off-grid lifestyle.

Trailers and RV Homes

Another option for those who don't want to settle in a single location is to live in a trailer or RV. It can also be a temporary housing choice until you find the perfect off-grid location or finish building your main house. RVs should be seriously considered since they allow you to take advantage of many modern amenities. They can be fitted with everything from a refrigerator toan air conditioner. You can also set up off-grid fixtures like solar panels to make this your off- grid home of choice. Another advantage of having an RV is that you can move it to an off-grid location or to the city whenever you want. When you want a change of pace, you can live in the area of your choice. You also can access free-use land in places such as Canada, where crown land can be parked for a few months at no cost.

Underground Home

If you want to try something really different, you might want to consider an underground dome house. These will require a whole lot of digging, and you might not get permission to live in these legally in certain places as well. However, these underground houses are a natural way of protecting yourself from very cold or hot weather. These houses also blend into the environment so seamlessly that a random passerby will not even notice it. There are a lot of people around the world who have built and live in underground houses like these. They are constructed in so many different designs, and you can try anything from a cave-like house to a fancy dome home. You can get creative and try different techniques to build a unique off-grid underground home.

Now all you have to do is choose the off-grid house of your choice and get a building or buy. Off-grid living can be as comfortable as you want, and you can be as self-sufficient as you want to be as well. There are so many things to experiment with and learn along the way. So, build your log cabin or explore underground living if you want. Consider your budget, needs, size of the house, etc., and start planning. Off-grid, housing is an adventure of its own. If you intend to live permanently on an off-grid property, try to invest a little extra time, effort, and money to build a more comfortable off-grid abode for your family to live in, in the long term.

Chapter Five
Meeting Nutritional Needs

One of the most important skills to acquire as an off-grid dweller is to grow your own food. While you may be used to running to grocery stores every other day or ordering takeout, theseare not options when you move to an off-grid location. The nearest store may be a few miles away at the least, and restaurants rarely deliver to such spots. More importantly, the whole purpose of switching to this lifestyle is to be as self-sufficient as possible.

What better way than to grow your own vegetables or rear your own livestock? You don't need acres of land to do this, but the more land you have, the better. You can work with whatever is available to you, and this applies to those who try off-grid living, even in their urban homes.Food can be grown anywhere from your balcony and terrace to your backyard. When you move to an off-grid location surrounded by nature, you have even more options and can forage or hunt.

This section will help you understand and learn more about meeting nutritional needs in off-grid living. It is not as simple as putting a few seeds into the soil and watering it. You need to learn about seasonal plants, good soil, drainage, watering schedules, storage, preservation, animal husbandry, and more. All of these are a part of proper off-grid living, and we will elaborate on each aspect of it to help you along.

If you've never grown a plant in your life, gardening and growing your own food can seem daunting. However, it is something you can learn easily with a little time and patience. You just need to be consistent, and you will literally see the fruits of your effort. In an off-grid garden,you have to consider your area's climate and what plants are suitable for it. You should also tryto grow more open-pollinated plants and produce that can be stored easily. Crop rotation, as well as succession planning, are other recommended practices. In terms of irrigation systems, you need to set up something that will be energy efficient since you won't depend on government power grids. Keeping all these in mind, let's get started with the know-how of growing your own food and rearing animals.

Choosing the Best Plants to Grow

Don't go to a nursery or store and pick up any random seeds or plants you see. You need to do some planning before growing anything in your off-grid garden. First off, what do you or your family like to eat? What is the climate in your area, and what plants will actually grow wellthere? How much do you need to grow to fulfill your needs? All these questions have to be factored in.

What Do You Like to Eat?

Make a list of the vegetables, fruits, etc., that you or your family like to eat. This is the best place to start, but don't limit yourself to these. From this list of favorites, you need to pick the ones that will suit your soil and climate. For beginners, it is best to start with plants that are not too demanding either. Now buy seeds or seedlings of these plants and plant half of your garden with them. In the other half of the garden, try growing other foods you may never have even tried. This will keep your diet filled with a variety of food and keep things interesting. You can try growing new things each season or year and avoid regrowing anything that you don't enjoy the first time.

What Climate Are You Living In?

The climate in your region will be suitable for certain plants and completely unsuited for others. You may find that potatoes grow well in your off-grid garden, but bell peppers don't. In a normal garden, gardening enthusiasts often try to push limits and grow plants unsuitable for their climate. However, such experiments are best left untried when you depend on your garden for your nutritional needs. It is best to first focus on growing plants that are sure to give you good results in your location. You can look at the government or local planting guides and ask your neighbors for advice based on their personal experience. This way, you will know what to expect from certain seeds and what you should ideally avoid for a while. In fact, asking neighbors or other off-grid dwellers in the area will be your best bet as compared to zone guides. You canlook at the records in your local library or historical society. This will give you information on what crops were naturally grown in your area in the past. You can uncover a lot of information with a bit of asking around and reading.

Work on Improving the Soil

Before you plant any seeds, work on improving the soil on your property. Fertile topsoil will make all the difference in determining whether your crop will flourish or fail. This is why soil building needs to be a priority for your off-grid garden. It can take a while to perfect it, but with each passing year, your topsoil will only get better if you work on it. If the soil is rich, theharvest will be just as lush.

Also, remember to start a compost pile as soon as possible. It doesn't have to be a fancy or complicated setup. You can simply pile it in a corner and allow it to compost. You can use some baling wire with a few pallets as well. Everything from eggshells to fallen leaves can be added toyour compost pile. You can add just about any organic matter into the pile. Just cover it with dirt and allow the composting to occur. If you notice the compost pile drying out, you can speed things along by adding a little bit of water.

Another tip for off-grid gardening is to try a no-dig and no-till method. Most farmers turn the soilover on their land, and this can destroy the natural structure. However, with no-till gardening, you will be improving the soil by adding more nutrients to the top each year. This improves the fertility of your garden soil and will give you better produce. More people are opting for this as opposed to turning the soil. Good soil can make all the difference, and you need to try anything possible to get a good harvest. Soil structure is very important, and that is very evident in all the lush natural forests around the world. They don't need to be watered and tended to as meticulously as a lawn garden because the soil structure is a lot better. If you apply the same principle to your off-grid food garden, you might see better results too.

Schedule Planting

Another important part of off-grid gardening is spreading your harvest well and maximizing how much produce you can store.

Early Harvest

When you make a planting plan, include early spring harvesting. You can do this by growing plants that tend to mature early. You can also do this by harvesting plants early before they mature if their younger forms are usable. For instance, green onions can be harvested in the early growth stage. You can take out the slower-growing plants and thin plant beds. Another trick is to harvest from plants even while they are growing. This is especially effective in herb gardens. If you only pick from the tips of the herb plants, it will promote fuller growth and actually gives you a better harvest from a single plant. This will give you a constant supply of fresh herbs throughout the whole season. Greens are also a great variety to include in your garden because you can try continual harvesting on them. Just pluck the larger lower leaves and allow the plantto continue growing.

Succession Planting

Planning your planting calendar in advance can be very advantageous. Keep growing on the garden bed throughout the year since it will help maintain soil fertility and structure. Soil tendsto get damaged if it is left uncovered for too long. Use the planting calendar to ensure that you have something to plant even after you harvest your summer crops. Succession planting can be done in two ways. One way is to direct sow, and another is seedling transplantation. In the latter method, you can start the seeds somewhere else and transplant the seeds directly into the soilafter you harvest the other crop. This will help you make the most of the space and start the second crop early. In the case of certain crops, you can grow them together in the same space.For instance, you can grow strawberries and asparagus at the same time since they mature and grow at different rates and don't have to be moved around. You can try other methods like guild planting to transform your off-grid garden into a whole ecosystem that gives you a constant supply of food.

Storage Planning

While food storage is a great way to keep a constant food supply, it takes a lot of work. Youdon't want to have to deal with multiple crops to store at the same time. Preservation methods take a certain amount of effort and time. So, plant your crops in a way that multiple storage cropsdon't have to be harvested at the same time; instead, you can do it one by one. You can adjust theplanting dates for such crops, so they mature at different times and give you more time to work on the preservation methods.

Irrigation System

You also have to build an irrigation system that is energy efficient. If you are providing for a whole family and need to grow food every year, it can be a lot of work to have to pull up water and do it manually. The best solution to such intensive work is to set up a watering system.

Gravity Fed Irrigation

Ideally, you should have a spring or river near your food garden. This is the best resource for an off-grid home that you should look for while selecting a property. You can then set up your garden at a water collection point downhill, and gravity will do the work for you. This is the simplest and most effective irrigation system. However, the gravity system will only work if the water source is above your garden. If the flowing water runs below your garden area, you may have to set up a hydraulic ram pump. This self-powered pump will help pump the water uphill with the energy from the flowing water itself. They are simple and can be built inexpensively.

No Irrigation Garden

If you live in a climate where it rains often, you don't need an intensive irrigation system. Just adjust the garden properly, and you can get by without irrigation systems. For instance, rainwater collection or berms can make your garden grow well by utilizing the water from summer rains. If the soil bed is well structured and has deep layers, it will retain water for a long time and allow your crops to grow well even without constant watering. Just make sure that you plant your crop with enough spacing, and that shade is provided. This will prevent excessive evaporation and the soil from drying out. This no irrigation garden can only be grown in certain climates and not in places where the summers are harsh, and there is hardly any rain.

Rainwater Irrigation

Rainwater irrigation can be utilized even in places where it rarely rains. The rainwater just needs to be collected and directed to a cistern, which can be used for watering your crops. Gravity will do most of the work if you set up the cistern on a higher level. If it is lower, you can set up a small electric pump.

Try to keep a few barrels in store for collecting rainwater. These are easily available in-store and online. These rainwater barrels will come in handy when you don't have access to any other water source. You can use smaller buckets to carry the water to the garden or for any other purpose. A spigot can also be installed and connected with a hose to water the garden. Use a mesh or screen to cover the top of your water barrels to help minimize any insect larvae or keep debris out. If you want to use the water for cooking or drinking, use a water purifier to clean the water first.

Protecting the Garden

When you move to an off-grid location, chances are, there is a lot of wildlife around. If you are growing food in your garden, they are also bound to be attracted to it. So, you need to take measures to protect your garden from wandering wildlife. It could be anything from deer to bears, so you need to take the appropriate measures.

Try some of the following steps:

-   Build a double-layer fence

-   Set up a fishing line fence

-   Keep a guard dog

-   Plant aromatic herbs like lavender

Seed Saving or Seed Crops

If you want to be completely self-sufficient in your off-grid home and garden, seed saving is an essential practice. Seed saving is the practice of harvesting seeds from the plants in your garden and using those to grow the next crop.

Choosing Plant Varieties

You can't grow hybrid plant varieties if you want to try seed saving. The hybrid plant varieties don't produce seeds that can be used for replanting, and others may not give consistent results. So, look for the labels on seed packets to check what kind they are. Heirloom seeds are a good option since they have resilient and disease-resistant properties. You need to grow plants thatwill give you seeds that can be planted and are open-pollinated. This is how you can get viable seeds for each planting season.

Planning For Seed Crops

Some of your garden space will have to be dedicated to seed production. Most seed-producing plants require a little more time after harvest so they can go to seed. You also have to notice ifthe plants have a tendency to produce seeds in particular seasons. Keeping all this in mind, some of your plants need to be for seed production so you can use them for the next season.

Raise Beneficial Livestock

While you might want to raise livestock for meat or dairy, they can also benefit your garden. Mixing the right animals into your homestead will help you take advantage of natural fertilizer inthe form of manure. The manure from domestic animals can be added directly into the gardenbed or into your compost pile. Either way, it will improve soil quality. Chickens are the best options for gardens since their manure is good for the plants, and they also act as a type of pest control by feeding on slugs or beetles that might eat your plants. Another option is raising ducks since they can help with slug control.

Crop Rotation

Crop rotation is another beneficial practice you need to include in your off-grid garden. It helps to ensure the long-term survival of your crops in many ways. One benefit is that it helps to prevent diseases from killing your crops. Another benefit is that it helps restore the soil fertility that might be depleted when you grow heavy-feeding plants. Some plants are very demanding on soil and tend to absorb almost all the nutrients from it. In this case, if you grow the same crop again after the first batch, it will soon render the soil useless. However, if you follow such crops with other crops that give to the soil instead, you can prevent this from happening. Guild planting is quite helpful in such matters but if you plan on growing the same plant, rotate the spot so the soil can be replenished. When you plant a heavy feeder in the first season, follow it with a giver and light feeder for the next. You can use plant guides to understand which plants are givers and heavy feeders.

You also need to keep in mind that replanting the same crop in the same spot year after year will encourage soil-borne diseases. This is commonly seen in the case of plants such as potatoes or tomatoes in particular.

- **Heavy Feeders** - Spinach, Squash, Radish, Beet, Asparagus, Corn, Pumpkin, Tomato,Strawberry, Broccoli, Celery, Cauliflower, Lettuce, Pepper, Cabbage, Rhubarb, etc.

- **Heavy Givers** - Peas, Soybeans, Alfalfa, Clover, Beans, etc.

- **Light Feeders** - Garlic, Onion, Sweet potato, Shallot, Leek, Carrot, Parsnip, etc.

Grow Beyond Common Crops

The more variety in the crops you grow in your garden, the better. This is true for various reasons. One important reason is that it will give you a better harvest, and another is that you willbe able to have more food for storage. When you pick seed catalogs, you should be able tochoose from a variety of different seeds with beneficial properties.

The details about each plant should be mentioned so you can plan your planting and harvesting times, storage, and more. Try growing as many types of plants as you can since it will make youa better gardener and also give you a varied diet. More importantly, don't just stick to growingthe crops that are commonly grown. You can also try growing your own grains, as you don'tneed to have a huge paddy field for this. A surprising number of grains can be grown in small batches and are suitable for different climates. Expand your horizons and learn about these.Some varieties you can try growing are oats, sorghum, quinoa, buckwheat, millet, and teff. The seeds are easy to source and not too hard to grow for a good crop.

Chapter Six
Productive Animals For Your Off- Grid Homestead

A completely self-sufficient off-grid home or homestead also involves raising some farm animals. You may never have raised an animal before in your life, and it can seem intimidating atfirst. However, if you start with a few and go from there, you will soon have a very productive livestock setup for your off-grid homestead. Don't buy too many animals in the beginning. Starting small will give you time to learn and reduce the chances of failure. Here are some of the best animals to raise on your off-grid property.

Chickens

The first choice for any homesteader is always chickens, which should also be yours. There are many benefits to raising your own chickens, and these include:

- You will have your own supply of fresh eggs and meat.

- They don't have a long lifespan and thus require minimal care compared to otheranimals.

- They are cheaper to purchase and raise than other animals.

- Chickens help to control pests and bugs in your off-grid garden.

- They can be fed scraps from your kitchen and garden.

- The manure from these birds can be used for fertilizing the garden.

- You are more likely to get a permit to raise these on your property even if other farmanimals are not allowed.

- They don't need a lot of space to keep.

- If you care for them well, they are not too noisy or smelly.

Chickens are raised either for meat or for laying eggs. You can also get birds that serve both purposes, but raising separate layers and meat birds is better. The latter is more productive and preferred by most. However, you can also look around for some good heirloom breeds that are dual-purpose birds. The meat bird varieties are a shorter commitment and will mature within 2-3 months. Egg-laying birds will give you eggs in about 6 months and can be productive for anywhere between 2 and 5 years, depending on the variety. You can also use the birds for meat once they stop laying or if you don't want to raise them any longer.

You will find that the meat from birds you raise in your own homestead will taste better sinceyou can refrain from using steroids and other substances that commercial breeders otherwise use. If you like making broths, you should raise some roosters or layer hens. Traditional recipes are often better suited for chickens that are raised on homesteads. So just check if your local authorities allow chickens to be farmed. If yes, ask your neighbors or look at local guides to lookfor reliable breeders to buy from. There are so many breeds of chickens to choose from as well that you will be surprised. Keep the coop clean and feed them on time; you barely have to do much else. Just remember not to crowd the birds in tiny spaces or wait too long to clean.

Bees

The easiest addition to an off-grid homestead is bees. You may think that raising bees will mean a lot of stings and swollen bruises, but this isn't true. Domestic bees tend to be very docile, and you won't need any fancy protection equipment. The benefits of raising bees are:

- It will promote pollination and thus increase productivity in your crops

- There are no daily chores to carry out with beekeeping, so it is very low maintenance

- They are a great source of honey for your home

- It is a free activity to carry out, and you just need some basic equipment

If you like adding honey to your tea or any food, beekeeping should be a must in your off-grid home. Organic honey is beneficial for health, and you can even sell it in farmer's markets if you want. The work involved with beekeeping is minimal compared to raising any other farm animals, and you don't need to keep checking in on them daily. The bees will also help to increase the production from your pollinating plants. Overall, raising bees will be another way you contribute to the ecosystem as well.

Goats

While bees and chickens are great for beginners, the next animal to add to your off-grid farm should be goats. Goats are considered all-rounders and have various benefits like:

- They are a good source of milk and meat

- Goats tend to be very resilient

- They are easier to keep than sheep or cows

- They need less space than larger farm animals

- Goats can be raised in most types of climates

- Goats also help to get rid of unwanted plants or bushes.

If you want to raise animals for milk and meat, goats are the best choice. You can try raising sheep or cows after successfully learning to raise a couple of goats. They are also useful for your off-grid garden since they can clear off most of the thick brush land. When you pick an off-grid property, you might have to deal with steep land, and this is especially easy to clear out with goats. Goat milk is a great alternative to cow milk and tastes really good if you cool it soon after milking the goats. You also need to realize that it can be hard for a beginner to deal with heavy cows as compared to smaller goats. It can be quite dangerous when you don't know how to deal with large, heavy animals, and starting with smaller ones is the smarter choice. The size factor also matters when you don't have too much land to work with. A smaller shed will work better with goats. If you are thinking of starting with sheep first, think again since it can be very hard to tell when they are sick, and you will just be left with sick or dead animals before you realize it.

Pigs

The best or most efficient source of meat for a bigger family would be pigs. You get a lot of meat and fat from raising a single pig, and this can be helpful for self-sufficient homesteaders. And another benefit is that you can turn the waste from your garden and kitchen into feed for them. Here are some reasons why you should raise pigs on your off-grid property:

- They will root in the ground and help clear the property
- Pigs will eat just about anything you feed them, including your kitchen and garden scraps
- They don't need too much space
- The meat from homebred pigs is very good quality, and you also get fat

If you are trying off-grid living in an urban area, it might be better to avoid pigs. However, in other off-grid locations, pigs should always be an addition to the livestock if you eat meat. For vegetarians or vegans, pigs would serve no purpose, unlike other animals that provide dairy. However, the manure from pigs tends to compost quite fast and is good for your garden soil. You can raise pigs to make your own bacon, ham, or sausages. These can be stored for longer periods in your freezer and gifted as well. So instead of buying meat at the store, raise your own pigs. Since a lot of commercial breeders feed their pigs unhealthy feed, you can rest assured that you get good quality meat from clean-fed pigs too.

Sheep

If you live in a place with a cold climate, you can raise some sheep. They thrive in coldertemperatures and are a good source of milk, wool, and meat. Some benefits include:

- They can be raised on pasture land

- They are docile and small animals as compared to cows

- Sheep are able to survive harsher cold weather

- The wool from your sheep can be a source of income or used for making things foryour own home

In the right conditions, sheep are a good livestock animal to raise. You get meat, milk, and wool and may even make money off their products. The cheese and meat from sheep is a rarity insome places, and you can sell them for a premium at the farmer's markets there. However, these animals are a little difficult to care for. You will need a full-time guard or dog to ensure that the sheep left to pasture are not hunted. You will also find it difficult to tell when your sheep need anything or get sick since they are too docile. A novice might easily find themselves dealing with a dead sheep.

Cows

Once you have more experience with farm animals, try raising a couple of cows. Almost everyone loves cow products, and if you do too, you should add them to your off-grid homestead. They take more effort and experience to manage but are ultimately worth it. Some benefits of raising cows include:

- Cow manure is very beneficial for improving soil fertility and growing better crops

- Self-raised cows will give you meat and milk of much higher quality

- It is cheap to feed them since they will pasture on grass for most of the year

You need more land to keep and raise cows, so keep taking that into consideration. The more pasture land around, the better since it allows them to roam freely and feed on the grass. But this is hard to come by, and it can be an expensive venture to raise cows otherwise. You can buy their feed and house them in a smaller cowshed, but this would be more expensive and ineffective. You also need to fence around your property to keep them from wandering out and around the garden and damaging the plants. Building a barn, buying milking equipment, etc., will add to the costs. This is why cows should only be raised by off-grid homesteaders with a higher budget, more manpower, and larger pastureland.

Geese

Although geese are often overlooked, they can be a really valuable addition to your livestock. Some reasons why you might want to add geese include:

- Goose eggs are large and nutritious

- They are a good alternative to raising turkeys

- You have a unique meat and egg product to sell if you want

- They will alert you in case of intruders and also help scare any predators away

A couple of geese can help protect your chickens quite effectively. They are aggressive and loud birds that can really do their bit. In fact, they were even used as guard animals in ancient Rome. When you are growing your own food, the more variety, the better; eggs and meat from yourown geese can be a welcome change to your usual diet. They are quite flavorful, and you can use them on thanksgiving instead of the usual turkey. Geese tend to be uncommon and can also be a unique product to offer at farmer's markets or restaurants. You can make a better sum from these birds than the usual chickens.

Ducks

Another kind of bird to consider raising is ducks. They are especially useful in gardens that have too many slugs around. The meat and eggs are very delicious and sell well too. The benefits of raising geese include:

- They are a unique meat or egg variety to offer at the market

- The eggs are large and tasty

- The meat is very flavorful and is a part of fine dining cuisine

- They are the best protection from slugs on your property

Although ducks are not very common, they can be raised without too much hassle. They are the best at removing or preventing slugs from ruining your plants. The meat and eggs are considered exotic produce in most places and sell at premium prices. You can just enjoy them for your own meals at a much lesser expense than paying at fine dining restaurants. If you have a pond on yourproperty, they are an essential addition to your off-grid life.

Quail

Quails can be grown for their eggs and meat. The meat and eggs from these birds are considered exotic in most places, but they are easy to keep. This is another good addition to your livestock ifyou want to sell unusual produce at the local farmer's market. While large animals such as cows need bigger properties and more effort, it is easy to raise these small birds. You can sell the meat or eggs to any fine dining restaurants nearby at a good price as well. This can be an easy side income opportunity in your off-grid lifestyle.

Fish

Many people miss out on raising their own fish, and you should try not to be one of them. These are one of the best additions to a self-sustaining, off-grid homestead. Here are some reasons why you should be keeping fish:

- Compared to other livestock, fish are quiet

- It is easy to get permits to keep fish almost anywhere

- They produce high-quality fertilizer for your land

- They are an essential component of a hydroponic system

- They are very easy to keep

- Fish are a very rich source of protein in your self-sustaining diet

- They are a good addition to duck ponds

If you have a small-scale off-grid farm, try keeping some tilapia and trout. These grow quickly and can be harvested soon. The meat is a healthy addition to your diet and can be sold as well. You have very little to do with fish when compared to other animals. They won't escape the enclosure and don't make a mess on the property either. They are a good source of natural fertilizer and will contribute to better crops. Planting row crops with moats is a common practice in Asia, and these channels are also used for keeping fish. This helps in the direct fertilization of the crops and also reduces bugs and mosquitoes. The fish can later be caught from the channels and consumed for meat. If you have enough land for it, you may also want to experiment with this method.

Rabbits

Rabbits are another easy animal to keep in your off-grid homestead. Some benefits of keepingrabbits include:

- They are child-friendly
- There is very little equipment needed to maintain them
- They don't make much noise
- Rabbits are legally allowed in most places
- Rabbits are a good source of meat

While you can't depend solely on rabbits for meat, they are a flavorful addition to your diet. Keeping a few different meat animals such as rabbits, chickens, ducks, or geese won't require too much space and are easy to keep for beginners. In the case of rabbits, you won't need to build any prominent structure to house them either. A simple cage is enough for rabbits, and these tend to be very cheap. However, you will have to clean the cages frequently to maintain cleanliness and avoid odor. Domestic rabbits are docile; you can help your children learn how to care for livestock using these as a beginner's lesson.

Chapter Seven
Food Preservation for Off Grid Dwellers

Off-grid living is its own kind of adventure, especially when you start learning how to grow yourown food or even go hunting for meat. However, an essential skill needed to live successfully off-grid is to preserve food. Food preservation is a life skill and a great practice to prevent food waste. It will see you through months of cold weather when you can't really grow any plants. It will also help you make your produce last longer when you grow more than you can consume at once. Food preservation techniques also help off-gridders keep their produce for selling at markets without spoilage. This section will teach you how to efficiently store or preserve your food in your off-grid home.

So, what are some food preservation techniques you should be familiar with?

- Canning

- Pickling or fermentation

- Cold box

- Root cellar

- Smoking or salting

- Fat storage

- Wood ashes or slaked lime

- Dry storage

- Honey

- Chest freezer

Food preservation or storage is all about finding a way to prevent wastage of any food you have spent effort and time growing for months. Food spoilage is usually caused by mold, bacteria, or fungus but can be curbed by keeping the food in conditions that don't support its growth. For instance, you can keep the food in very cold or very hot temperatures. You can also preserve the food by adding too much salt or sugar or immersing in very acidic or very basic solutions. Similarly, drying food is another great way to preserve it by removing moisture.

Canning

You have probably bought canned beans or fruits at some point in your life. This practice ofcanning is one of the most basic yet effective food storage or preservation methods. As an off-grid dweller, you will find canning to be one of the most useful skills to learn for the long term.

So, what do you need for canning?

- A pressure cooker or canner

- Glass jars

- Airtight lids for the jars

- A canning table book

The traditional metal lids on canning jars are usually not reusable but are quite cheap and can be bought in bulk. However, if you want a more sustainable choice, buy canning lids that aremarked for indefinite reusability. These are easily available in the market at slightly higher pricesthan the usual metal lids.

The basic principle behind canning is that the food will be partially cooked and stored in an airtight jar, so no harmful microorganisms are present or able to enter and spoil the food. The storage jar itself will be sterilized or boiled to kill anything that might potentially cause the food to spoil. In the case of canning, the main safety concern is botulism. Botulism is a disease that is caused by bacteria such as Clostridium botulinum and can be quite harmful to humans. These bacteria are able to thrive in low oxygen environments and thus can grow inside canning jars too. However, they don't do well with sugar, salt, or highly acidic conditions. This is why botulism is usually not an issue with jams or salsa. However, for canned foods such as meats or vegetables, you will have to sterilize the food at temperatures high enough to prevent any chances of botulism.

Having a reliable canning guide will help you use canning in the right way for different kinds of foods. This will help you prevent any errors that might cause your canned foods to spoil or cause illness. There is a lot of information on canning instructions online as well, and these resources can be invaluable for an off-grid lifestyle.

Smoking, Salting, or Drying

Smoking, salting, or drying are some of the common ways in which meat is usually preserved. However, these methods can also be used to preserve many vegetables and fruits. The main principle here is to reduce the moisture content in these foods as much as possible to reduce the risk of spoilage. Moisture allows microorganisms to thrive and thus helps them spoil the food. The salt or acidity also prevents the growth of such microorganisms. However, unlike fermentation or pickling, no liquid solution is used here.

In the case of salting meat, it will generally be kept in a cool and dry spot where the meat will cure. You can have a separate curing room or do this on some rafters in a shed outside. For smoking, you might have to build a smokehouse or smoker. Meat can be smoked by cold smoking or hot smoking. When you use hot smoking to dry meat, the meat also gets cooked during the process. This is why the meat is not stored with hot smoking. Cold smoking uses cool smoke to cure the meat and is thus used for preserving meat. While many people also use preservatives, it is not a traditional practice. Salting or smoking meat also dried the meat out. The salt will draw moisture out from the meat, and smoking does the same. Low heat will have to be applied if you want to dry fruits or vegetables for storage, so the moisture is drawn out. This can be done in a solar dehydrator, low-temperature oven, or just by spreading them out on a surface under the sun.

Cold Box

A cold box is a simple off-grid method of refrigeration. Storing food in cold temperatures is one of the most common ways of preservation. While almost every modern home has a refrigerator, you might want an alternative form of it for your off-grid home. Instead of relying on power or electricity with a refrigerator, you can try a cold box. A cold box is simply a well-insulated spot in a shaded area of the house with a small opening. This opening would allow cold air to go in during the summer and help preserve foods that otherwise perish easily in hot weather. In the winter, the cold box would prevent the foods from freezing but still keep them cold for preservation.

Ice Box

A low-cost icebox is another option to consider. These are insulated boxes with a block of ice and have been around for ages. Before people had access to electricity, they would buy ice from an icehouse and put it into the box. If you live in a colder climate, you can make your own blocks of ice over the winter and store them for use during the summer. If not, you can buy the ice or build an icehouse on your property. An icebox helps to prevent a lot of food from spoiling due to heat.

Chest Freezer

You can still use a freezer or refrigerator in your off-grid home if you have some power source. However, it helps reduce pressure on your power source if you also have a chest freezer. These chest freezers work well with solar power and can be used for freezing anything from meat to vegetables.

Chapter Eight
Meeting Water Needs

Figuring out how to meet water needs in an off-grid home is another essential aspect of preparation. There are a lot of opinions and experiences, and you might be a little confused abouthow to figure this out for your own home. You have more options than just a well or sticking to the local water supply. This section of the book is meant to help you understand how off-grid water systems work and what all your options truly are. It will help you make a well-informed decision and set up an effective water supply for your off-grid home.

So, in general, off-grid water options include:

- Deep wells

- Surface water from creeks or rivers

- Shallow wells

- Rainwater collection

- Gray water

When you are building or buying an off-grid home, you will see that setting up the water system might actually be one of your biggest expenses. This will depend on the choices you make forthe water system. However, you shouldn't skimp on it since it is an essential need for you and your family. You will need water for drinking, cooking, bathing, cleaning, and, more importantly, for growing food in your garden.

In terms of water supply for off-grid homes, you need to consider a lot of things. Water systems are rarely a concern in urban areas since builders usually set them up. You only have to pay the monthly water bills to ensure running water. The local water system provides everyone with water through pipelines, and water can also be bought easily. However, when you go off-grid, you might not want to depend on these providers. Depending on where you move, you can explore different water supply options. It can be a bit of a hassle compared to city living, but it is all a part of self-sufficient living.

How Do Rural Homes Generally Source Their Water?

A deep well and septic tank are the most common ways for rural homes to get water these days. However, they are expensive to set up since they require heavy machinery, and you will have to hire professionals to get the job done. The laws and building codes vary from place to place. However, a lot of places will require you to get the septic and deep well installed before you start living there. There are also limitations on how many people can live on a property, depending on the size of the septic tank. You will have to look into the laws in your state before you move into a property and start building. However, some states also have provisions for other alternatives, such as pit or composting toilets that many off-grid dwellers use.

Why Should You avoid Installing a Deep Well?

While deep wells are a common option, you might want to avoid choosing this as your water source. The water from a deep well is sourced from a sealed aquifer. This is why the water is considered safe to use, unlike shallow wells. The water is just pulled up in a shallow well with a rope and bucket. However, a deep well is dug a lot lower in the ground and comes from below a layer of clay. This deep-sourced water reduces the incidence of surface chemicals and microorganisms that might otherwise be an issue with shallow wells.

The water from a deep well has been underground for hundreds of years and is a lot cleaner. However, the expense of getting a deep well set up is quite large. The depth of the well cannot beestimated prior to the actual digging process. The more they have to dig in, the more expensive the process. Deep wells require special machinery for drilling since they are usually a few hundred feet in depth. The cost of digging a deep well can be anywhere between $1000 and

$10,000. This will depend on the depth of the well as well as the professionals you hire. Deep well drilling is regulated in most places, and you may have to get a permit from the local authorities before you dig one. Look into the local regulations and get the essential paperwork sorted to avoid any issues in the future. You may also find that your request is rejected, and this will affect your ability to water a larger garden in particular.

Powerful pumps are required for drawing water from such depths, which are also expensive. They are also very energy consuming. This, in turn, will mean you need a bigger solar power system or any other energy source. It will affect the cost of setting up energy for your off-grid home and will require a larger budget. If there is a glitch in your power supply or the pump doesn't work, you will also have to have an alternative water source ready. Deep wells draw water from aquifers, which are gradually shrinking, so avoiding them is best. The water is getting used up in excessive amounts, which will affect the water supply in the future.

Why Should You avoid a Septic System?

First off, a septic tank is a large underground tank that stores human waste and sewage from homes. These are installed in homes that aren't connected to municipal sewers and are usually made of concrete or fiberglass. While most septic tanks have some filtering system to allow liquids to seep underground, it will depend on where you are. The design of the septic systemand the soil on your property will affect this. This is why you may need to hire a truck that will pump the sewage content and take it to a treatment plan. This will mean that you still use on-grid services and are not completely self-sufficient. You will have to pay a certain fee for availing of this facility, and it can add to long-term costs. The cost of the actual tank itself is also quite expensive and can range anywhere between $10,000 and $25,000 depending on the size, type, etc. This is why we don't recommend a septic tank for a good off-grid home.

Alternative Water Systems for Off Grid Living

So, if not a deep well and septic tank, what should you try using for your off-grid home? First, you need to check with the laws in your state since a deep well and septic tank may bemandatory. If not, then you can try any of the alternatives we recommend here. You can also use these as supplementary sources along with the deep well and save money and resources this way.

Rainwater Collection

One of the best ways to meet water needs is rainwater collection. It is quite inexpensive and requires very little tech to set it up. Rainwater collection is allowed almost everywhere in some form or other.

The amount of rainwater you will be able to collect will depend largely on the amount of rainfall your region gets. This may vary from year to year, as well as the climate changes. The size of your collection structure and your roof will also be determining factors. If you want to have an estimate of how much rainwater you will be able to collect, you need to make a few rough calculations. One way is to multiply the area of the collection surface or roof by the inches of rainwater that you expect to get. This quantity can then be converted to liters or gallons to understand how much water you can expect.

Another thing to consider is what the size of your storage needs to be. Consider the seasons in your location and what periods you don't get much rain at all. The water storage unit should be large enough to help you get through these dry periods and meet most of your water needs. For instance, if you don't expect rain for 4 months of the year, you need to store water for those months. The amount of water stored needs to be even higher if the rainy season isn't during the growing season. For regions with summer rains, you won't need as much water storage and can easily get by with smaller facilities. Purification is required if you intend to use the collected rainwater for drinking or any other domestic use. A filter needs to be installed, and you also need a first flush diverter. Rainwater collection for off-grid homes is further explained in a later section.

Shallow Wells

Shallow wells are one of the oldest methods for acquiring water and are a lot simpler to build than deep wells. The water in these wells is drawn closer to the surface, unlike the deep underground water pulled in deep wells. However, there is a bigger chance of contamination in the case of shallow well water. In fact, a lot of states don't allow shallow well digging anymore, so you need to check with the local authorities for your options.

If you are allowed to dig a shallow well on your off-grid property, you can try hand digging. There are a few different ways of digging this kind of well, but a common method is to use water-based drilling heads. These are known to work well in soil, which has easier access to surface water like sandy soil. You can even use a rotary auger. It is used to dig out the dirt and form a well-hole. This auger is then pulled back out, and the debris will have to be removed. Depending on the type of soil, you can try digging a shallow well using different methods. Since the chances of contamination are higher with this water, you will have to test and purify the water, especially before consumption.

Surface Water Sources

Other alternatives are water sourced from streams, lakes, rivers, or springs that might be located around your property. If you are lucky and have access to these water sources, you should definitely take advantage in a sustainable way. These are great sources of water for irrigating your garden, but you need to purify the water properly before using it for drinking or cooking. Like shallow well water, this is surface water as well and has high contamination risk.

Another factor to consider is if you are legally allowed to use the water from these sources. The laws and regulations may vary from state to state. In most states, you will legally be allowed to use water from sources that pass through your property or are adjacent to it. However, in some states, you may have to apply for rights to use this water for whichever purpose you intend. The water rights in your area may also be suspended or prohibited if there is a drought or any water issues. So, before you buy a property, you need to check with the local authorities. If it is allowed, make sure to get the required permits.

Off-Grid Water Storage

If you want to collect rainwater for your off-grid home or need to store water for fires, a cistern will have to be installed on the property. These large water storage tanks can be quite expensive, but they are an investment worth making. You will be assured of having stored water for use when other water sources are unavailable, and this is quite important when you live away from urban facilities.

The following are some options for water storage in off-grid homes:

Poly Tanks

Poly or plastic tanks come in various sizes, and smaller ones can be inexpensive. However, the largest ones of certain types can be more expensive. They also need to be protected from the sun since plastic can break down with excessive UV light exposure and release chemicals into the water. This can make the water unsuitable for use and degrades the tank. The tanks have to be given some cover or buried to protect them from light exposure. You can also buy tanks that are built for outside use but adding protection will make plastic tanks last longer.

Galvanized Steel Tanks

Galvanized steel tanks are more expensive but can last

longer than plastic tanks. They are usuallyused for storing 1000+ gallons of water.

Stainless Steel Tanks

Compared to any other option for water storage in an off-grid home, stainless steel tanks are probably going to be the most expensive. However, they are the most durable type of tank and don't involve the use of any plastic either. This makes it a preference for health-conscious peopleand those who intend to make an off-grid settlement their long-term abode.

Clay Cisterns

If you are especially environmentally conscious, you can build a water tank with cobs. This would be a mixture of clay, straw, and sand and would be lined with tadelakt. Tadelakt was originally used in waterproofing surfaces in Moroccan bathhouses but is now used widely in natural building communities. It is a mixture of soap and water with impervious lime. These tanks are eco-friendly, inexpensive, and non-toxic.

Chapter Nine
Off Grid Water Purification

If you aren't digging a deep well or sourcing water from urban facilities, your off-grid water sources will usually be prone to contamination. This means that purification is an important aspect of meeting your water needs. Here is some information on water filtration in an effective yet cost-efficient way.

Water Contamination

Water can contain a lot of harmful contaminants that need to be removed. Any kind of water can be potentially contaminated, so you will be responsible for filtering or ensuring that your family has clean water. There are 6 main types of water contaminants that you need to be wary of:

- Fluoride

- Heavy metals

- Radionuclides

- Nitrate and nitrite

- Microorganism

- Organic chemicals

You can buy drinking water test kits to keep a check on the water used for consumption. Kits in different price ranges are available, but you should do your research and choose the better qualityones to ensure health safety. Other than these DIY kits, you should also allow professionals to come and test your water periodically. Getting professional testing is a more reliable option that will also give you peace of mind.

Building a Bio-Filter

A bio-filter or sand filter is a cheap and easy water purification option. These are great forgetting rid of any sediment and for removing weird tastes from your drinking water. However,the disadvantage is that it will not remove heavy metals or bacteria from contaminated water. They also help when you want to improve hard water or soft water. These bio-filters can be used as an additional layer in a ceramic or UV purification system. Bio-filter is a great last step to implement in a chemical disinfectant system too. If you have a deep well, you can use this as an extra step to clean the water.

There are three layers in bio-filters:

- The first layer is gravel.

- The second layer in the filter is sand.

- The last layer is activated carbon or charcoal.

Gravel and sand are physical filters that will separate any large sediment from the water and allow it to settle in the sand. The activated carbon or charcoal is the layer that will help toremove chlorine, fertilizers, organic chemicals, etc., from the water.

Activated carbon is charcoal that has been processed with high-pressure steam. Charcoal used for water filtration should always be from a clean source. You can also choose not to buy it commercially and prepare it on your own property by burning any waste wood or brush.Charcoal is very reactive since it is mostly composed of carbon and reacts well with water. You can choose to use basic charcoal or go the extra step to prepare activated charcoal. In either case,the charcoal used in the filter should always be finely crushed.

So, how do you build this bio-filter?

It is easy to find or buy sand and gravel for the first two layers of the bio-filter. However, you should always wash them thoroughly before actually using them for filtration. Now use a food- safe container for making the filter. For instance, a 5 or 10-gallon bucket can be used. Cut holes into the top of the bucket and another hole into the bottom of the container. Now get a good pipe for the water flow. It will have to be glued in a way that water enters at the top and comes out through the hole at the bottom. Now you have to create the bio-filter. First, add the charcoal layerand follow it with sand. Then you can pour in the layer of gravel. The thickness of your bio-filterlayers and the area of the filter will determine how much water you get. About 10-inch layers of each of these materials should be enough. If you need more water, use bigger buckets. You will get more water to use per day if you use wider buckets with a larger surface area. Like anything else, maintenance is important for bio-filters as well. Bacteria may grow in the bio-filter, so you will have to clean it out completely from time to time. The carbon, sand, and gravel layers can then be replaced so you can use the bio-filter again. Doing this once a year is usually enough.

Building a UV Water Purification System

Dirt or debris is a physical component that can be easily removed from the water. Since they are visible, you can easily tell when the water is cleared of such contaminants. The main cause of concern is always bacteria or other microorganisms that can cause illness. If your greatest concern is water-borne diseases, you might want to try a UV water purification system. It is a cost-effective purification system that is easy to build and use. In fact, a lot of commercial water purifiers use UV light for this same purpose. UV light is known to effectively kill the most harmful bacteria and is used for sanitation across various industries. The light frequencies destroy DNA and cell structures and thus help remove harmful viruses. However, the light alone will not be enough since it cannot remove physical debris from the water or remove chemical contaminants. This is why you should combine it with other sediment filters like charcoal or ceramic filters.

To build the UV water purification system, you need to choose the right bulb first. All UV lights will not work the same or serve your intended purpose. To disinfect drinking water, you should use UV bulbs ranging between 200 and 300 nm. The nanometer denomination will tell you the frequency and wavelength of the bulb. In fact, you may just opt for 260 nm bulbs since theyseem to be the most effective. Don't pick up a light bulb just because it is labeled UV since this nanometer measure is more important and will be listed on the packaging. However, rememberto take the proper precautions when using these bulbs since they are potentially harmful to you aswell and can cause damage to the eyes and skin.

Once you get the UV bulb, you can directly insert it into the lid of your water bucket orcontainer. The normal bulb should ideally be as close to the water surface as possible but waterproof ones are your best option. You also need to ensure that the bulb gives off enoughlight to illuminate the entirety of the inside container. If there are any corners the light doesn't reach, there is still potential for bacteria or harmful microorganisms to survive there. There should be no additional material between the light and water since it will affect the effectiveness of the process. Even transparent materials can block the UV light, so don't add such layers to protect the bulb. The only material that can be used without blocking the UV light is quartzglass, but these tubes can be very expensive.

So how long does the water need to be exposed to the UV light radiation before it can be considered purified? The total time required will depend on the amount of water as well as the frequency of the bulbs. This means that the UV exposure and the area will determine the time. According to the EPA, 2.5 mW s/cm^2 is recommended for at least reducing cryptosporidium. Accordingly, you need to figure out how much time you expose the water, depending on how much water you need to purify. A few minutes is usually a good idea and will sterilize yourwater container.

An alternative to this is the simplest form of UV purification, which is exposing the water to natural sunlight. Direct sunlight exposure for a few hours can be used for sterilizing water in an open bucket or basin. You cannot do this with water in a transparent plastic or glass container since they will still block the UV rays. It will only work if the water is completely exposed to direct sunlight and kept there for several hours at a time.

Ceramic Water Filtration

A ceramic water filter effectively cleans and disinfects water when it passes through the microscopic pores in the clay. The minute pores don't allow microorganisms to pass through, andthis separates them from the water molecules that do go through. Ceramic water filters are also very easy to set up since you can easily buy the parts. You can also make your own ceramics if you have the skills or tools. However, it might be easier to opt to buy the ceramic candle replacement filters and get them installed in your water purification system. Check the reviews for various ceramic filters and get the one that lasts longer, even if it is initially a little expensive. Good ceramic filters can last longer than a decade and are worth the investment if you can get clean drinking water every day in your off-grid home. Some filters also have activated charcoal cores for further purification and help improve the water's taste. Silver cores do the same and are very effective but cost more. These are not necessary additions and only add to the cost. However, you may choose from any of the different ceramic filters in the market based on your budget and intended use. Remember that this filtration method is quite slow, and you will have to allow the water to filter for at least a day before you can get the required amount of water. You will also need multiple filters depending on how many people you need the water for.

It is quite simple if you want to build and not buy a ceramic filter system. Just stack a couple of water containers together first. Now measure the size of the filters. Cut holes into the top of the upper bucket so they will be the right size for the filters. Screw the ceramic filters in through the holes on the top bucket. The unfiltered water can be poured on top and allowed to filter through to the bottom bucket. You can insert a spigot or pipe into the bottom bucket and use the filtered clean water.

Chemical Disinfectants

If you are looking for stronger disinfectants for the water, consider using chemicals. As you may already know, bleach or chlorine can be added to help disinfect water. However, they should always be used in appropriate amounts. This chemical disinfectant method is widely used worldwide, from large-scale projects to home projects. Similarly, you can also use it to purify the water in your off-grid home.

It is a simple process if you want to use bleach to treat the water on your property. All you need to do is calculate how much bleach to add according to the amount of water. For each gallon of water, 1/8th of a teaspoon of bleach is sufficient. Mix the bleach into the water and stir well. Allow this mixture to sit for 30-40 minutes for the disinfection to take place. Once this is done, you can use the water for drinking or cooking. The water may not taste very good with this chemical disinfectant, but it is one of the quickest DIY solutions. You can opt for other water purification methods for your main source, but having some bleach in storage can be handy. Bleach is also useful for a lot of other DIY purposes in off-grid homes, so it won't go to waste. If you use a bio-filter for purifying your water, you can use bleach as the first step before passing the water through the filter.

Distillation for Water Purification

Distillation is another method you can employ for purifying drinking water in off-grid homes. This process uses heat for water purification. The water is first heated until it turns into steamand then cooled to condense it back to liquid, which is collected in another container. This method allows the removal of any dirt particles as well as harmful microorganisms and bacteria. It is one of the most effective ways of cleaning water.

A DIY and simple way of carrying out distillation would be to heat the water on a stove and collect the steam from condensing it in another container. However, it would require a lot of timeand be expensive since you would have to boil gallons of water daily. But this is only viable if you want to purify small amounts of water at a time.

If you want to use distillation as one of your main methods of water purification, you should invest in a solar still instead or make one. These can be prepared in a few different ways, butmost designs involve a plastic or glass sheet with water underneath. The exact system will be a bit different in these designs, but the main principle of distillation remains the same. Solar stills are a great option for people living in hot climates since you get access to a lot of direct sunlight throughout most of the year. You can use solar stills quite effectively if the conditions are right. You can also fully automate it if everything is installed properly.

Boiling for Water Purification

In off-grid properties, there can be a lot of situations where you need to have a backup ready. Itis even more important to have alternatives here since you don't have access to urban utilities as easily. In the case of water purification, the easiest alternative for an emergency is to simply boil the water. It can be done on a stove or even over a campfire. The water should be brought to a rolling boil for a couple of minutes before you can consume it. If the water seems dirty, you can use coffee filters or a muslin cloth to clean it and collect the sediment first. This purification method can be used in a pinch but should not be used as the main method.

Chapter Ten
Meeting Power Needs

Figuring out a source of power is essential in off-grid living, especially if you want to disconnect from the grid. You can try anything from solar panels to wind or water turbines for this. This section will give you an idea of how to set up an efficient power system for your off-grid property.

Off Grid Solar Energy

Solar energy might be the best thing you invest in, and it really isn't as difficult or expensive to set up as you might have imagined. Here's a comprehensive guide to getting started with off-grid solar energy.

The following steps will give you an overview of what building a solar system will involve:

- Determine your power requirements.

- Pick the right location.

- Pick the components.

- Build a battery house.

- Install solar panels.

- Wire the system up.

- Use the free solar energy.

Designing Your Solar System

When you want to design a solar system for your off-grid home, the first thing to remember is your power needs. You will save time and money if you follow the process step by step instead of skipping over important parts. Another important thing to remember is that the energy needs in your home may change with time. Solar energy panels or any other renewable energy source will not be able to provide consistent results throughout the year, and you need to factor this in as well. This is why it is crucial to determine your family's power needs so you can find a way to ensure they are always met, regardless of the variables.

Pick the Right Location for the Solar Panels

Once you determine the power needs, you need to pick the right place to set up the solar power system. You may think that it makes the most sense to set the panels up on the roof, but this is not necessarily true. Other spots around your property will get the same or more exposure to sunlight, and you also have to find a spot that is easily accessible. You should be able to access the solar panels without having to climb your roof every time, and the spot should also allow the panels to passively cool as needed. If you can find a spot that allows this, you can make the panels last a long time and work twice as efficiently.

Picking the Components

Once you know the power needs and find the right spot,

you will be able to pick the right components for the solar setup. Ordering the right components is important since they will work more efficiently for your needs. When you do this step, there are a few different things to consider:

How many and what size solar cells will you need? What is the rating of the inverter?

What voltage do you need to pick for each leg, and

should they be AC or DC?

What kind of charge controller should you be using?

What is the battery type and battery bank capacity?

Components of a solar power system usually include:

- Misc. connectors

- Battery bank

- Fuses and disconnects

- Copper wire

- Solar panels

- Charge controller

- Inverter

Build the Battery House

After you place an order for the solar power components, you can start building the battery house. This can be a separate shed you build for this purpose or even a room already existing in your off-grid home. Solar batteries need quite a bit of space, and you also need to make sure they are placed somewhere that animals or even kids won't reach them. They can be damaged and dangerous if not placed correctly. Another thing to remember is that most solar batteries need a certain amount of temperature control. Keeping them in a spot where they are exposed to freezing temperatures may spoil the batteries. You can get batteries on different budgets, and the cheaper ones will require you to add ventilation in the battery house. This will prevent hydrogen gas from building up, which can lead to a dangerous explosion. The cheaper batteries tend to release this gas over time while charging, and you need to be careful while using them. It is also better to have any of your power electronics placed in the battery room since it will reduce costs. This can include anything from your inverter to the charge controllers.

Install the Solar Panels

Let's talk about installing solar panels. You need to build the support for the solar panels before proceeding with the installation of the solar array. Ideally, the panels should face the sun directly. On receiving direct sunlight, they will be much more efficient and in turn, provide far more solar energy. It is also important to remember that constant overheating will damage the solar panel setup. The panels will last a lot longer if they are cooled properly. The support structure can be built in a few different ways. You can do this depending on whatever materials you have available or can afford. Your skills will also factor in, but you can hire someone for the initial set-up. Use a wooden or metal south-facing A-frame if you want the maximum output from your solar power system. For higher efficiency, make it manually adjustable. This will allow you to adjust the tilt of the panels according to the seasons and thus ensure maximum efficiency. While installing the solar panels, these few adjustments will increase your power output by almost 40%.

Wiring Up

Once you set up the solar panels, you have to start wiring up. This is not a difficult task since an off-grid power setup is less complicated than a grid tie system. Off-grid homes can usually function with a completely DC system, which is much simpler to install. However, an AC system can easily be set up as well. One thing to keep in mind is that if you choose to stay connected to the usual power grid and want to add a solar system as well, you will need to hire a professional electrician. It is a legal requirement in almost any place to do this since the utility company will need to provide other hardware to allow both power sources to work efficiently together.

Determine the Size of Your Solar System

If you want to figure out how many solar panels you need, you first need to determine the amount of energy you will be consuming.

How Can You Measure the Amount of Power You Use?

To determine your required power usage, you should measure it by yourself using a power- measuring device. It is inexpensive and can be used with any of the appliances you plug intoyour home. The kill-a-watt device just needs to be plugged in along with your appliance, and it will give you certain measurements. You have to keep track of the kilowatts or watts of energy used. You can set the kill-a-watt to get readings in kilowatt-hours. Ideally, you should keep it plugged in for a day to estimate how much energy is used per day. Another option is to plug it in for an hour and then multiply the kilowatts into the number of hours you use per day.

How to Calculate Daily Usage

Using the kill-a-watt, you can get an estimate of how much energy each device in your homeuses per day. Now you need to add up all these energy measurements to get an estimate of the total energy usage in your home per day. However, you also need to keep in mind that the energyyou use daily will fluctuate throughout the year. For instance, you will only use a heater during the winter months, and you won't use the lights as much during the summer when the days are longer. Try to make adjustments to your power usage estimate by keeping the different seasonsin mind. It can hardly be accurate but will give you a better idea about power usage than assuming that the energy consumption is consistent throughout the whole year. For an off-grid dweller, it is important to know how power usage will vary through the year since the amount of solar energy produced will also vary. In the winter, with shorter days, the amount of sunlight reduces, and so does the solar energy produced. The amount of sunlight and thus solar energy is more during long summer days. So, you need to ensure that the solar panels you install can give you enough power for any of the seasons.

Determining the Amount of Solar Energy Produced

As mentioned above, the amount of solar energy produced is greatly dependent on how much sunlight the panels receive. The solar power output will greatly decrease on winter days or even when the sky is cloudy. The maximum amount of solar energy will be produced on sunny days, especially during the summer. Thus you cannot get the same amount of sunlight for generating solar power on all days. The best way to determine the actual amount of solar energy produced is by measuring it. Before you set up an entire solar power system, measuring this will be very helpful. You can buy a single solar panel and set it up on your roof. Now, use this to measure the amount of energy it produces through all the seasons in a single year. You can do this while preparing to make the off-grid shift, even in your current urban home. This way, you will be able to know how many solar panels you need to install in your off-grid home. However, the climate or seasons can always vary, and it is always best to install a few extra solar panels to make sure you don't fall short on solar energy at any point. This is especially important for those who intend to go completely off-grid and don't want to stay connected to the power grid. You can also get a lot of information on solar power from government data, so make sure to look it up.

Size Up Your Solar System

You now need to choose the right size for your off-grid solar system. This will help you ensure that you have enough power for any season in the year. To ensure this, you might have to installa larger system than a smaller one and thus have more power than you need for many months. You also need to understand that getting a larger system helps because solar panels are not always completely effective. There is power loss involved in the entire process as power is transferred from one component to another. You can try to determine the efficiency of each component of your solar system and then determine the number of solar panels to install. However, this can be a bit of a hassle, and instead, you can choose to keep a 70% figure in mind.

Now you just need to calculate how many solar panels you need according to the kW energy required by your home and divide this by 0.7. Keep inefficiencies in mind as well, and this will give you an idea of the size of the solar system you should install.

Battery Capacity

Solar energy is only produced during daylight hours when the panels get exposed to sunlight. At night, the solar system will run with the help of batteries. These batteries are also important for cloudy days to help provide enough power even if there isn't enough sunlight. The minimum requirement for battery capacity is that they should be able to store a day's worth of charge for a winter day.

If the solar system in your house produces about 1 kWh per day, the battery bank should be able to at least store that much. The capacity of batteries is measured in Ah or am-hours. So, you need to multiply the Ah by the battery voltage to determine kilowatt-hours. The general batteries available and used range between 12V - 24V and 48V. The latter is more suitable for solar energy systems. You must also familiarize yourself with the different types of batteries available. For instance, lead acid batteries of any kind will only have a certain amount of discharge depth. So, you will need to determine the number or size of the batteries while keeping such factors in mind.

Where to Install the Solar Panels in Your Off-Grid Home

For most people, the common choice for solar panel installation is the roof. However, you will find that your home's roof is not always ideal for this purpose. There are a few reasons why you might want to reconsider this usual placement on the roof. One factor is roof direction, another is the ease of access, and the third is shading.

Ensure that the panels are placed at the right angles. If the placement on the roof doesn't allow the solar panels to face the south, you will lose out on a lot of potential solar power generation. The right angle for the panels will also affect the amount of solar energy being produced. If your rooflines don't already face the south, it can be difficult and expensive to fix the panels appropriately.

Solar panels should always be accessible. Solar panels need to be kept clean and cooled down so they can have a long life and work with maximum efficiency. It is natural for any dirt or dust to accumulate on them, so you will need to do some cleaning as often as possible. However, if you place the solar panels up on some inaccessible spot, this will be a difficult task. Snow, in particular, can be very damaging for your solar panels. So instead of putting the panels on the roof, place them closer to the ground. This makes it much easier to clean off dirt or snow routinely. Regular maintenance will allow the panels to work efficiently for your home for a longtime.

Avoid shading. This is another extremely important factor to keep in mind. Your solar panels should not be obstructed from sunlight in any way. So, keep them away from any tree or buildingshade. In fact, even a little bit of shade has a massive impact on solar power production. If the solar panels are under shade instead of being exposed to direct sunlight, the power output can reduce by almost a third of what the system would otherwise produce. So, the panels should be placed on your roof or house if it is completely devoid of any shade above. If not, try to place the solar panels in another spot near the property where it will get full sun exposure. The wiring of the panels will also be factored in, so you might reduce the power output even more due to the wrong placement of the panels.

Solar panels do not function well when they get excessively heated. They will wear out fasterand will produce a lot less power in this case. However, placing the panels in a way that there is at least a 6-inch gap behind them for airflow will allow better cooling. Roofs tend to be hotter than most other spaces, and this makes it harder to keep the solar panels cool. Some people use mounting racks on the roof, but you can save money on this if you focus on correct placement instead. Just try setting up the solar panels in another cooler spot.

So, avoid placing the solar panels on the roof but keep them as close to the house as possible while ensuring that they get full sun exposure.

Hydro Electric and Micro Hydro in an Off-Grid Home

Solar power is not the only alternative option you have. You can consider and try hydroelectric and micro hydropower as well. Micro hydro is a consistent source of power and is not very visible either. All of these things make it a viable off-grid power option.

So, let's assume that you want to increase the amount of micro hydro or free waterpower you have. The most important aspect of tapping into free water for power needs is choosing the right off-grid property. If you find a property with a natural water source, you will then need to get water inlets, outlets, a penstock, and a turbine house constructed. Then you have to choose the best turbines, cost-effective but functional generators, and proper electrical connections.

Once you do all three things, you can start the micro hydropower setup.

Each of the steps mentioned above is a whole process and key to the functionality of the micro hydro system you will want. Depending on your needs, you can use it to supplement your main power system or even as the main power source.

Choosing the Placement of the System

When you set up a solar power system, you can easily increase the amount of power you get by adding more panels and batteries. In a micro-hydro system, the amount of water flowing will determine if you can tap into waterpower in the first place. If you want to tap into a stream running through your off-grid property for power, it needs to have a drop of at least 5 ft. If not, you cannot generate energy from it for your home. Another point to remember is that you will have to depend on the whims of nature while using such alternative systems. If the water flow suddenly reduces or stops, it can cause problems. The placement of the inlet and outlet will play an important role in helping you get the maximum amount of energy from the system. An inlet is where the water from the stream will enter the system, and an outlet is where the water will be driving the turbine. The pressure of your micro hydro system will be determined by the altitude decrease from this inlet to the outlet. This pressure will then help you decide on the appropriate generators or pumps to add to the system. The pressure and the flow rate will then determine what the maximum amount of power you can generate from this system will be.

The inlet and the outlet will have to be placed so that the maximum drop is possible since this will help you generate more power. However, to do this, you might have to spend more on the penstock piping as well as any supporting structures that might be required. You can use larger piping if there is a lot of water available from your water source. Even if the pipe runs a short distance, the same amount of power could be generated, and this will be done with the minimal extra expense.

What Is a Penstock?

A penstock refers to the piping that runs between the inlet and the turbine within the system. Any common piping can usually be used for this purpose, but you should invest in the kind that is meant for external use. Plastic is susceptible to degradation if it is exposed to sunlight for too long. It should be covered so it can last for a longer time. While buying the penstock, check if it is rated such that it will be able to effectively handle the water pressure and weight. This water pressure flowing through the penstock must be maintained consistently. It is also important to prevent any leaks in the pipe. If there is a leak or a loss of pressure due to any reason, it will directly cause a reduction in power output from the micro hydro system.

Determining The Amount of Water Power That Can Be Generated

Even if you want to try using micro hydropower, you need to figure out whether you will be able to generate enough power for your needs. This will depend on the drop from the inlet to the outlet and the amount of water flowing through your off-grid property. Determine the pressure

and flow rate from the stream, which will allow you to calculate the power you can generate with a micro-hydro system. Just multiply the flow rate with the pressure to determine power output. However, the value you get from this calculation will give you the estimated maximum power. Once the system starts running, you will get less power than this value. If the numbers seem too little, it might not be a reliable source of power for your off-grid house.

Measure the Available Pressure

First, you need to measure the available pressure or head to calculate the final power output. The simplest way of doing this is using a pressure gauge with a garden hose. Connect the pressure gauge to the garden hose, and it will easily give you the pressure of the water flowing through.

- Take the pressure gauge and garden hose to the site of the inlet.

- Now submerge the garden hose

    and ensure that all the air goes

out first. Screw the pressure
gauge into the hose by following
the given instructions.

- The gauge will have to be extended to the potential outlet or turbine site.
- The end of the hose that is open should be kept submerged in water.
- Now read the measurement displayed on the pressure gauge attached.

You can also try heat-based measurement. The drop from the inlet to the outlet is very long; measuring it directly is easier. All you need is the exact distance between the two. If the drop from the inlet to the outlet is a straight drop, you can use a tape measure. You can use a GPS for very high inlets to measure steeper inclines. This pressure is not the actual distance between yourinlet and outlet. It is just the up and down change in altitude. Now multiply the distance by 0.434, and you will get the PSI pressure measurement.

Measure the Flow Rate

You also have to measure the flow rate of the water. If the water source is small like a small stream running on your property, you can use the bucket method for measurement. It is used by good drillers quite commonly and can easily be done. You will need a timer or a watch and a few 5-gallon buckets.

- Set the timer or your watch for one minute.

- Start the timer and place the bucket under the source to collect water.

- While the timer is still on, keep switching the filled bucket for an empty one.

- Count how many buckets are filled before the timer goes off after a minute.

- Now multiply the number of buckets into 5, and this is the gallons per minute or flowrate.

You also have to remember that the flow rate will differ throughout the year depending on the season. It can increase during heavy rains or when the snow melts. It can decrease at some point too. It will help if you measure the different flow rates during each month of the year. It will also give you an estimate of the lowest flow rate you may expect in the next few years. This can be useful information in determining all your calculations.

The Weir system is used for calculating flow rate in the case of larger streams. For larger sources of water, the bucket system is not as reliable. To use the Weir system, you will have to construct a low dam with a flat top, and the water will flow over this. It only requires a little bit of digging and filling. Once you create the dam, measure the width of it and also the depth of the water flowing over the top of this weir or dam. Use this to get the flow rate of the larger stream.

How to Construct a Micro-Hydro Inlet

Now that you have the pressure/head and the flow rate, you can start constructing the inlet. This will be the most expensive and time-consuming part of the process of setting up a micro hydro system. Pipes or weirs will have to carry the water from the water source to the turbine and back. The micro hydro inlet can be a simple installation of a wooden box that has a stream to filter out debris. This will prevent any dirt from blocking or damaging the turbine, which is quite expensive. The inlet screen should be placed perpendicular to the flowing water. This will allow the water to keep flowing naturally while filtration occurs. If this inlet is not designed and installed properly, it will later affect your entire micro-hydro system and prevent sufficient power production. Before moving to the next part of building the micro hydro system, ensure that the inlet is working efficiently.

How to Build the Penstock

After the inlet has been constructed, you can build the penstock of the micro hydro system. This penstock will usually just be a long pipe running from the inlet to the turbine. The most straightforward option is to pick a PVC pipe of the right size. In some micro hydro systems with low heads, an open canal can be employed directly from the stream to the turbine. However, most of these systems need a larger flow rate to justify the expense of setting up the micro hydro system. If a large river runs through or near your off-grid property, you can depend on it to be a good source of hydropower.

In general, the expected flow rate will determine the size of the PVC pipe for the penstock. You can refer to the recommended pipe sizing charts that help you choose the right size according to the expected pressure and water flow rate. These are easily found online or in books on hydropower. For instance, a 6-inch PVC pipe for 100 PSI would be enough for a small household. If the size of the pipe is a little too big, there will be no negative repercussions. The only con will be that it will cost you more than a smaller pipe. However, the pipe should not be of a smaller diameter than needed so it can handle the expected water pressure. Oversizing the pipe will also give you the chance to increase the capacity of your micro hydro system in the future. This could be a wise decision when setting up a penstock since it can be expensive to redo later.

The Difference between a Buried and Above Ground Penstock

Penstocks are not always placed above ground. The penstock of a micro hydro system can also be buried underground at times. Each of these placements has pros and cons for you to consider before setting up the penstock.

If you want to bury the penstock, you will have to spend more time, effort, and money digging and carrying this out. It will also make it more difficult for any maintenance work to be carried out. For instance, if there is a leak in a pipe, you will have to do a lot more work just to get to it. However, the advantage of a buried penstock is that it protects the pipe from exposure to strong sunlight or even damage from any fallen tree. If the pipe is left exposed outside, it will become brittle and damaged over time from sun exposure. In the case of an above-ground penstock, the installation process is a little easier than burying it. Depending on how the water runs, you may have to build some extra support structures. This will ensure that the water runs freely throughthe pipe without losing pressure in a straight flow. You also need to consider that most PVCpipes are not meant for exterior use, so you will have to add an extra layer of protection from UV exposure. A layer of latex or acrylic paint will usually suffice. However, you can't use oil paint for this purpose. Either way, the penstock installation is a little complex regardless of whether you choose to bury the pipe or keep it exposed outside.

Building the Turbine House

Building the micro hydro turbine house does not have to be as complicated as you might expect. The turbine can be stored outside in a simple shed. You can easily construct one with leftover wood or any recycled material. You will not have to install any heating in this shed unless you live in freezing temperatures. However, heating will help if you want an emergency stop feature for the micro hydro system. This will prevent the turbine from freezing or cracking due to very cold temperatures. These turbine houses are usually built very close to the water source since it helps minimize the amount of pipeline required for the penstock. The further the turbine house, the longer the pipe will have to be to direct the water there and back. If your area allows you to use the water for other purposes, you can also set up the turbine house in a way that the used water is directed to your crops for irrigation or the house for other purposes.

Picking the Best Turbine

These days, a lot of turbines are available on the market for setting up small-scale hydropower systems. These are usually rated for power generation and marked for the recommended flow rate and pressure. You can use this information to choose the most suitable turbine for your off- grid micro hydro system. Instead of choosing one bigger turbine, you might want to pick acouple or more of the smaller turbines. Setting these up together will be cheaper than buying the larger ones. It will also allow you to prevent a complete power failure even if one of the turbines fails. So, buy an extra backup option and keep it ready. If you depend on a single large turbine, itcan be expensive to get it fixed, and you will also be struggling to meet your power needs until the issue is resolved. While there are tutorials on building your own DIY water turbine, investing in a commercial one is best. This will reduce the chances of error and be worth the money in the long run, especially if you choose this as your main power source.

Picking the Right Generator

A generator or alternator is rated by the power output type, intended voltage, and maximum size. You will have to pick the generator rated for a minimum of the power that you have designed your micro hydropower system for. If you have a 2 kW system, you should pick a generator with at least a 2 kW rating. You can pick larger generators, too, but not smaller ones.

The design of your micro hydro system will determine what kind of generator you need. In off- grid homes, you will usually have to convert the output from the generator to DC, as you will probably be supplementing a solar power system with the hydro system, and most batteries are DC devices. It is the best choice to use the highest DC voltage for the generator, which ranges around 24-72 volts DC.

If you don't intend to use the waterpower just as a supplementary source, you can run the system directly on AC power. Since you won't have to power any batteries or backup, DC will not be required. Now you can choose between a 120 and 240-volt AC. AC power systems are a good choice since they are very efficient and simple. As long as you don't intend to use devices that require heavy electrical load, this will work well. You can run easily on AC micro hydro systems in a simple off-grid home with lights and basic devices. However, you might also want to hook on heavy load devices such as motors or big appliances to the generator. In this case, you need to make sure that the machine turns at 60 hertz, or your appliances will easily be damaged. This can be achieved with a little active electrical control to keep the water flowing at a constant rate.

Keeping all this in mind, we recommend a DC micro hydropower system. This will allow your power system to efficiently handle more complex electronics. Try adding wind or water generators with controllers but ensure that the attached charge controller has the option of attaching a dump load. The spinning turbine should be connected to a load when there are fully charged batteries. You can also connect a second load if you buy a higher-end charge controller.

Using Hydropower with a Grid Connected Power System
If your off-grid home is still connected to the grid, you can also use a micro-hydro system. To do this, a grid-tie inverter will have to be installed to allow the generator to work alongside the grid power. Some states even allow you to sell excess generated power back to the main grid. You will have to check with the local authorities and power companies to see what is allowed in your area. The required permits will have to be attained, and you may also have to hire a professional to get the installation done.

Depending on the details, a micro hydropower setup can cost

anywhere between $1200 kW and

$9000 kW. Consider your power needs, the capacity of the available water source, and your budget before setting up a hydro system. However, it is generally a good option alongside solar power systems for permanent off-grid homes.

Off Grid Air Conditioning

If the summers are really hot where you live, it can be difficult to survive without air conditioning. If you install an air conditioner in an off-grid home, it can be very expensive to run these units on solar power. So how do you keep cool in an off-grid home without spending too much money?

Here are some options:

- Swamp cooler

- Earth cooling

- Absorption coolers

- Solar-powered wall air conditioner and heat pump

- Ancient roman style water cooling

With these methods, you can stay cool and still be self-sufficient. You don't have to use the traditional air conditioners for this and do it at a fraction of how much you would be spending.

When people consider putting a normal air conditioner in

their off-grid home, they don't realize just how much power it will have to draw. It means that a much larger solar power system will have to be set up, which can immensely add to the power costs. Even a smaller air conditioning unit will consume at least 1000 W, and central systems need more than three times this amountof power. During the summer, if you run this system for a few hours a day, think of how much electricity you will consume. If you want to run a small AC wall unit, it will cost a few thousand dollars in panels alone. So, you can install the AC with your solar unit if you want, but you need to know if it is a financially feasible option. Instead, you can try smarter alternatives that will cost you a lot less and are not as complicated either. If you think about it, air conditioners were only invented a couple of decades ago. People still found ways to stay cool before installingthese modern machines in their homes. So, it is definitely possible for you to stop relying onthese power-consuming machines as well.

Passive Solar Design

These work well for off-grid houses. This simply means that you find ways to prevent yourhouse from getting heated due to excessive sunlight exposure and thus won't need an air conditioner. There are various ways to do this. You can take advantage of things such ascovering vegetation or implementing proper window placement during construction. These smallsteps should be taken while constructing or setting up the house, and they will help protect you from harsh weather. You can also use thermal batteries for leveling out the temperature throughout the day or night. If you look at homes in most tropical countries, you will see that their traditional designs tend to keep such things in mind, and they are less dependent on air conditioning than in western countries. It can be fairly simple to keep your off-grid house cool and comfortable. Just work on a good design for the house and try using thick earth walls.Simple hacks at the time of construction make a world of difference.

Earth Cooling

One of the best alternatives to cooling your home is using the earth, which acts like a thermal battery. The temperatures underground tend to stay consistently near normal room temperature throughout the year. This means that an underground cave will often be the same comfortable temperature throughout the year, regardless of your climate. This is the principle that most Earthship buildings have been taking advantage of for the last few decades. They were originally built in New Mexico. These days, people all around the world have been adopting this technique.The Earthship houses are built in a way that a large earth mound makes up the north part of the house. Along with this, air transfer ducts are also built in. The earth mound is thus a big thermal battery for the Earthship house acting as an insulator and protector for the inside of the house. A lot of modern buildings in hotter climates have been adopting this earth cooling technique in their construction process. They are called earth-coupled heat exchangers and are basically just long tubes that are buried into the ground to transfer heat from the building into the groundbelow with the help of water or air.

Absorption Coolers

Absorption air conditioners are one of the more new developments in this field that can greatly benefit off-grid dwellers. These units aren't based on compressors or Freon like the regular air conditioners. Instead, they are built using much safer and cheaper materials. These absorption coolers have a lot of potential for effective use in houses with solar power systems. Most of the energy used in cooling with these machines is obtained from heating water. This can be provided at no cost by using a solar water heater. While development work on these units is still being done, there is a lot of potential for them to work more efficiently and cheaply than traditional air conditioners.

Water Cooling

For people with natural sources of running water on their off-grid property, it becomes even easier to maintain cooler temperatures in their homes. It could be a river, stream, or spring running into or near your property. If you have access to these, you can try the ancient Roman technique of water-cooling your home. In ancient Rome, the nobles or richer families were allowed to access the Roman aqueducts for water. They could divert water from there into the walls of their houses, and this would help keep the inside of the house cool during summer. Even if you live in a modern home, you can still implement this water-cooling method.

Install in-floor radiant heating loops using heat exchangers and fans. If you choose the latter, you should adapt the plumbing to the cool water source on your property.

Solar-Powered AC Unit

If you still choose to stick to the regular air conditioning unit for your off-grid home, you can still connect it to a solar power source. You can consider running it solely during the daytime with no battery systems involved or connect it with direct DC solar units. Batteries factor into one of the highest expenses related to off-grid solar power. You can save money if you run the air conditioner directly with solar panels. The air conditioner can only be used during the hours when the sun is out in this case, but it will save you a lot of money. Since you need the AC more during daytime hours anyway, this can actually work out. You can also buy a direct DC unit that runs without an inverter and instead just runs with solar power. Inverters are expensive, to begin with, and cause wastage of energy during conversion.

Swamp Coolers

These are a popular cooling option in summers since they are quite low-cost. Evaporation of water is used for cooling a space using swamp coolers. However, the disadvantage of this method is that they also cause increased humidity levels. Due to this, you might not want to use a swamp cooler inside your home, but you can use it for the shed you keep livestock in during the summer months. It can be a cost-effective way of keeping the animals from suffering in the heat outside. Swamp coolers are also used in the form of mist sprays in gardens or outdoor spaces to cool the air around. This makes them especially popular during the summer months when people want to spend some time outside but are looking for a way to cool down.

Passive Solar Design

Passive solar design can be used during an off-grid home's remodeling or building process. It helps you keep simple principles of cooling masses and shading in mind so the house will stay cool. This way, you won't have to depend on power-dependent machines to cool the house. It saves a lot of money in the long run when you use passive solar design while building the house.

One of the main aspects of this is managing how sunlight falls into the house. In most places, people rarely give a thought to sun positioning while building their house. However, if you consider the climate and position of the sun throughout the day, you can figure out a way to build the windows in the most appropriate places. With careless window positioning, you will actually be setting up your home to get excessively heated from the sunlight entering through them. With the right solar design, you will be able to face the windows of your house towards the east or south. While this will protect the inside of your house from excessive heat, it will allow more insulation in the colder sections of the house and better heating during colder months. It is also important to have the right length of eaves so the entire window can remain under shade during peak afternoon hours. However, they should also be built in a way that they allow enough sun to enter during the winter daylight hours for natural warmth.

If you already have a house with poor solar design, you can benefit from using plants as living shade. Growing vines along the house's walls will help reduce direct sunlight from heating the inside. Instead, you will be able to save money on cooling requirements. You can also plant deciduous plants around the west side of the house to provide more living shade and keep the house protected from too much sun. During the winter, the leaves will fall naturally and allow the sun to provide warmth to the house. In the summer, the leaves will allow cooling again.

Thermal batteries are another way of maintaining normal room temperatures without needing to spend too much on cooling with an AC. You can do this by opting for construction methods such as earth bag or cob building. They help to keep the inside of the off-grid home, similar to how caves stay cool inside. In a stick frame house, you can add thermal mass using Trombe walls. Implementing passive solar design in such houses with earth floors is also easy.

The better the insulation value of the off-grid house, the better the passive solar design will work. You can do this in many ways, including the use of insulated doors or double-paned windows. You can also add more pink foam to the walls or try better weather stripping.

Alternatives for Septic Systems in Your Off Grid Home

Since septic systems can be very expensive and leave you dependent on third parties, you might want to consider alternatives for this. Septic systems handle gray water and black water in off- grid homes. The gray water is slightly dirty water from showers, sinks, etc., and the black wateris dirty water from toilets. You might want to handle these wastewater types differently in your off-grid home to reduce costs and increase waste management efficiency.

Gray Water Management

A gray water system is a plumbing system that manages the gray water from the sinks and showers in your home. It includes storage, filtering, and discharge of this lightly soiled water. There are a lot of designs for gray water management ranging from complex to simple systems. The complex ones will usually involve the use of commercial filters and tanks. The simple gray water systems can be as easy as using a pipe to direct the dirty water to a biofilter set up outside. The biofilter can be made by growing filtering plants in layers of sandy soil. The discharged water will then go back into the environment with minimal negative impact.

If you don't pour any toxic substances into your sink or drain, the gray water can sometimes be used for watering plants. However, this should only be for plants that won't be consumed. You can water flowering or non-edible plants safely using gray water. Some plants can be used for cleansing the gray water as well. If this water is acidic, you can grow plants such as rhododendron or ferns with it. Similarly, check the quality of the gray water; if it's okay, you can use it for watering suitable plants but if it's toxic, you can't.

A gray water system is designed so that the water can be reused and discharged back into the ground. In order to do this, you have to avoid using some chemicals and cleaners that will make this water too toxic. Avoid using any bleaches or products meant for softening or whitening. Youalso need to avoid any cleaners with boron, chlorine, borax, oxygen, alkylbenzene, etc. Look for products that are best for gray water systems and more sustainable for the environment.

Alternative Toilets for Off-Grid Homes

Handling human waste properly is essential to setting up an off-grid home since it can otherwise cause unsanitary situations and be harmful. You get black water when water mixes with human waste, and is called sewage. You can direct the waste down directly into the soil for an off-grid alternative to septic systems and public sanitation. Storing black water and dealing with a septic system is more complex and will require you to call service providers from time to time. This option will be lighter on your wallet and also helps in improving the soil quality on your off-grid property.

To install alternative waste management systems or toilets, you need to check the laws in your area. In some places, a permanent settlement requires installing a septic tank. In others, you may be allowed a particular type of alternative toilet but not another. There are places where youwon't be restricted by too many waste management regulations, which gives you more room to try different types. However, you must remember that waste always has to be handled properlyto prevent toxicity issues and maintain a hygienic environment for your family and you.

Biogas

Biogas is a very important development in the sustainable waste management field. The basic principle of biogas is that waste is stored in an airtight tank where it ferments in an oxygen- deprived environment. Certain microorganisms thrive in such environments and these will then decompose the waste to produce methane and compost tea as products. The major advantage of this waste management alternative is that the methane can be utilized in heating and cooking. However, after it is produced within the digester, the methane should be filtered to remove any contamination or smell. The filtered gas then works like natural gas and is thus an alternative fuelsource for off-grid homes too. Another advantage of setting up a biogas system is that you can add animal manure from your homestead and any other combustible material as well. Germany has used this system for decades since it helps them generate electricity on commercial farms. Many small homesteads have been trying this, too but it isn't as widely used yet.

Humanure

Another alternative to consider is humanure. It is a system of waste management where human waste will be composted directly. It is extremely cheap to use this system and also very simple to carry out. In the first part of this system, you will be using a dry toilet with a biodegradable cover and odor arrest. The manual handling of waste involved in this makes it a process some people don't want to work with. The toilet is moved to a compost pile outside whenever it is full. The composting process also helps to improve soil quality in the long run. Waste buckets will need to be moved outside almost every week or even twice a week if they are small in size and multiple people are using them. Proper handling can minimize or remove any foul smells from the waste.

Composting Toilets

These toilets work similarly to humanure systems. The difference is that they can hold a lot more waste for longer. There are many kinds of composting toilets that range from large permanent toilets to smaller portable ones. The operating modes between these systems also differ, so you can choose from different kinds. Since most toilets have separators, the liquids are automatically separated from the solids. The liquids can then be moved or transported outside through pipes to decompose. The frequent improvements made to composting toilet models make it easier for users since they won't have to be emptied as frequently. Most models also have agitating systems so the waste will automatically be flushed after every use as it disperses cover material. This is why these are easier to manage and generally preferred over the manual handling of humanure systems. It is especially more convenient after you have been used to the normal flushing toilets in modern homes. However, the con of this system is that it is a lot more expensive. The portable models can cost up to $1000, and the permanent toilets cost upwards of $1000. Even if you optto go the DIY route and build a concrete composting toilet, it will cost a lot. Thus, this option is suitable for off-grid dwellers with higher budgets.

Chapter Twelve
Living Off Grid without Buying Land

While most of the book has focused on buying your own off-grid property, it is not the only option when choosing this lifestyle. You can go off-grid without owning land, too, and that is definitely another option to consider. You may not have too much money in the bank, and we don't recommend taking out huge loans for an off-grid home. If you get a bit creative or want to try any of the ideas mentioned here, you can go off-grid without emptying your wallet.

Rent a House or Land

You can avoid buying land and committing to it by just renting instead. This is a good option for larger families or someone who doesn't want to live in a tiny home. You can get more space without spending money on buying a large property. It will be a bit more expensive than a tiny home but not as much as purchasing a property. Some benefits of renting include:

- You get more space to live in.

- There are fewer issues with neighbors.

- You have more freedom to do what you want.

Invest in owner-carry land. This is a good option for someone who wants to start a larger homestead and have more control without buying a property outright. The benefits of having an owner carry land contract are:

- You don't have to worry about being told to leave the property.

- You get a lot of freedom to carry out any homesteading activities you want.

Land Partners

If you think you can share land, you can find a partner or two to buy the off-grid property with. This land-sharing practice is quite common in some places and is a lot more feasible than buying the whole property with your own money. Try doing this with friends or family you trust or who have the same interests. There are actually a lot of people who would love to try off-grid living but have financial constraints. You can get a legal contract to share the property together and continue with your off-grid lifestyle.

Communities

If you are a social person and can get along with groups, try being part of intentional communities. This will allow you to live with other like-minded people and also give you the option to try different kinds of off-grid communities. You may even be able to trade the right to use the land in exchange for work.

Building or Finding a Tiny Off-Grid Home

If the thought of a tiny home appeals to you, you can buy or build one. There are many listings online and in local papers that you can look through. You could rent, buy or build one as per your preference and budget. The thing about tiny living is that you need to be more minimal and cannot afford to hoard stuff anymore. With limited space, it is necessary to live with the bare necessities as far as possible. Many manufacturers sell tiny homes these days, and they are available in different types and sizes. If you are good with your hands, you can try building one yourself. It is a bit of time and effort but will only make you more self-sufficient. Building your own tiny off-grid home is actually the best option since you can work within your budget and build according to your personal preferences. Another tip is to approach any local wood shops or construction sites to see if they have any extra materials. You may even find a lot of perfectly usable materials lying around in certain places or being sold at throwaway prices.

Renting Off-Grid Land

Due to laws, off-grid homes are usually not available for rent as full-time residences. However, you can rent a place and just choose not to use the utilities there. You could also rent bare land and live in winter; the leaves will fall naturally and allow the sun to provide warmth to the house. In the summer, the leaves will allow cooling again.

Conclusion

Thank you for making it to the end of this book. I hope you have learned enough to get started with off-grid living in a much more confident manner than before you began. You might also have realized that it would not be the best lifestyle choice for you, and that is an informed decision that might be best for you.

Off-grid living is not as difficult as you may have expected, but it takes a lot of work and commitment at first. So, take it step by step and utilize the tips given in this book. Decide on the degree of off-grid living you want to undertake and go from there.

Find the best location suited for you and establish yourself and your family there. You can be self-reliant and comfortable at the same time. You don't have to compromise on either. Off-grid living is much like a camping trip but a long one that is better in many ways. If you've ever felt like you didn't want to return from a camping trip, off-grid living might be perfect for you.

This book has probably helped you understand all the good and bad aspects of off-grid living. Now you can utilize all the information to start your journey to living off-grid!